SUPPORTING
Autistic Girls
& Gender Diverse Youth

An essential neuro-affirming
guide for parents, teachers & allies

(✱) greenhill

https://greenhillpublishing.com.au/

Yellow Ladybugs (author)
Supporting Autistic Girls & Gender Diverse Youth
ISBN 978-1-922957-35-1
SELF-HELP

Typeset in Myriad Pro 11/18
Management by Ginny Grant
Illustrations by Chenai Mupotsa-Russell (Rainbow Muse), cover and throughout, and Em Hammond (Neurowild), pp 57 and 221
Foreword by Katie Koullas
Book design by Green Hill

FOR KIKKI, MIA AND ALL THE
YELLOW LADYBUGS AROUND THE WORLD – KK

Contents

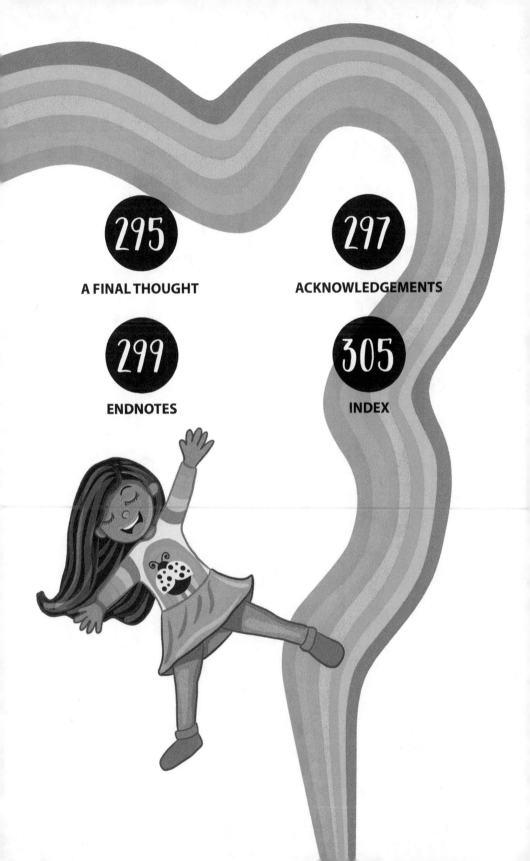

In the spirit of reconciliation Yellow Ladybugs acknowledges the Traditional Custodians of Country throughout Australia and their connections to land, sea and community. We pay our respect to their Elders past and present, and extend that respect to all Aboriginal and Torres Strait Islander peoples today.

We also recognise our inherent advantages and privilege, and wish to reject any reinforcement of our present hierarchies. Our privilege does not mean we live a life of ease, but it does mean we have historically, systematically and practically experienced fewer obstacles than our Black, Indigenous, and people of colour (BIPOC) and our Culturally and Linguistically Diverse (CALD) neurodivergent community.

FOREWORD

This is the book I wish I'd had, all those years ago. The guide I wish I could have turned to, when I felt so alone, so lost, trying to understand this new world of autism, we had suddenly landed in. Little did I know that autism has been part of us, part of me, part of my family history, well before its more formal introduction. It is maybe the reason why it became my intense passion, as I deep-dived into this magical new world of realisation, and created Yellow Ladybugs – to unite, connect and find our people.

As the founder and CEO of one of Australia's largest autistic-led charities, I am really proud of the community my wonderful, mostly neurodivergent team and I have created, and the impact we have made. We have been on the frontline of advocacy and change for those of us with a more internalised autistic presentation. We have had the opportunity to reach millions online, sharing from our lived experience with our own brand of authenticity, love and genuine care. I am proud that we are making a change, not just for our children, ourselves and our community, but in honour of all the generations gone by who were not understood, not supported, accepted or celebrated. We do this for them. We owe it to ourselves. We do it for the future generations, who may walk a better path than ours. I have always wanted to share what I have learned on this journey, and take the collective wisdom from our wise, insightful and generous autistic community, and pass it to each of you.

So, when an opportunity came up with the Victorian Department of Education to publish an autistic-led and informed book, I knew exactly what it needed to be.

It needed to teach. You will learn so many new things – hello, information overload – with a good combination of evidence-based content and lived experience.

It had to connect. You will fall in love with our incredible autistic community, who will share their personal stories with you. You will also find anonymous stories from neurodivergent parents peppered throughout the book, because we want to keep it real with you and give you insight into what the world can be like parenting as a neurodivergent adult.

It must inspire change. We hope this will encourage teachers, parents, health professionals and allies to re-think how they support autistic girls and gender diverse students. We will challenge you and guide you to approach things differently – always upholding our philosophy of being a safe place to turn to, trauma-informed and neuro-affirming.

You will be able to use this book in a way that works for you. Some of you might read it from top to bottom, back to front. Others may jump straight to the quotes, interviews and diary entries from our neurodivergent community. Others can go straight to the index at the back to find exactly what you need. Either way, we hope you get a lot of value from it and share what you have learned with your own community, so we can send ripples of change into the world.

Thank you to the collection of neurodivergent authors, who have collaborated with me in creating this guide for you, including Ginny Grant, Alisa Mlakar, Jodie Simpson, Shadia Hancock (Autism Actually) and Gilly McKeown (Neurodivergent Researcher). Many thanks also to the fabulous illustrators, Chenai Mupotsa-Russell (Rainbow Muse) and Em Hammond (Neurowild).

Before I conclude, I thought it might be good to understand what inspired Yellow Ladybugs and offer a bit more about our story. Feel free to jump straight into the Introduction if you have heard this all before, or if you are keen to just get started. Yellow Ladybugs wouldn't exist without one special young ladybug: my daughter. She was having a rough time at school. Invitations were few and far between. So, we both decided to throw a party. She wanted to invite other girls like her, who may be missing out on invitations or play dates. She was going make them her guests of honour, and she was going to name her new club after her childhood special interest – yellow ladybugs.

We had 20 girls come along to our first event, with some travelling from as far as three hours away. It was incredible. We saw the parents looking on, with tears in their eyes, as their ladybugs (in their yellow t-shirts, headphones and messy hair) were playing freely and laughing together. I knew this was our new mission, our new adventure. I knew that we could make a real difference. I didn't know at the time what neurokin meant (autistic peers) or what autistic culture was (check out our last chapter on this) but on a basic level, I knew we had found our people. That's what we are all about, and what we have been all about ever since that wonderful day in 2015.

We have hosted thousands of ladybugs at autistic designed and delivered events. It still gets me teary seeing how safe each ladybug feels when they come along to be celebrated for exactly who they are. As I discovered my own neurodivergence, our work evolved and grew. We have fiercely advocated for systemic change and become leaders in neuro-affirming education. We have proudly provided a much-needed platform for autistic people to share their story, hopes and vision for a better tomorrow. And now we step into a new frontier. On behalf of an incredible team, we give you our first-ever book, and we hope it provides you with everything you need and more.

xoxo Katie

INTRODUCTION

If you're reading this book, chances are you're a parent, caregiver, teacher or other support professional who is keen to understand more about the autistic girls or gender diverse youth in your care and wants to help them to thrive. Or perhaps you see your daughter or gender diverse child struggling in various ways at school or at home – or both – and are wondering if they might be autistic. Either way, we are so pleased to have you on this journey with us: autistic happiness, success and celebration is central to our mission at Yellow Ladybugs.

First up, there are a couple of housekeeping matters. Regarding language, no doubt you will notice that we use the term 'autistic' in this book; as in 'I am autistic', rather than 'I have autism'. This is known as identity-first language or IFL, and it is the strong preference of the autistic community,[1] as we feel that autism is an integral part of who we are, rather than some kind of add-on or accessory. We also use the term 'autism' on its own, without the full medical diagnostic term 'autism spectrum disorder' or 'ASD', as we see autism as a neurotype – simply as a neurological difference

– and not a disorder. You won't find 'ASD' anywhere in this book, or indeed, in anything else Yellow Ladybugs does. Secondly, while we have a particular focus on autistic girls and women at Yellow Ladybugs, we are an inclusive organisation. We recognise all genders and warmly welcome trans and gender diverse autistic individuals into our community. We also consider that the different presentations of autism exist across all genders, and as an organisation, we seek to dismantle all stereotypes which are harmful to the autistic community. So, it is for this reason that we have used the terminology 'autistic girls and gender diverse individuals' throughout this book.

Finally, you will see the word 'we' crop up from time to time. To be clear, this 'we' refers to the writers of this book – autistic adults themselves, who bring a range of lived experiences to the project. When talking about autistic people, it is vital to include diverse authentic autistic voices in the conversation. As the saying in the disability rights community goes, 'Nothing about us, without us.' In the following pages, we begin by providing a definition of sorts, an explanation of how we see autism, give a snapshot of its prevalence, discuss the hidden or internalised presentation of autism that is so often found in our ladybugs, and explore some of the key aspects of being autistic. In Chapter 2, we delve into aspects of an autistic girl or gender diverse individual's home life. Chapter 3 focuses on the specific challenges faced by our ladybugs attending school. In Chapter 4, we look at some of the co-occurring mental health issues affecting autistic girls and gender diverse young people. Chapter 5 explores the important subject of healthy relationships, gender and sexuality. And Chapter 6 looks at the concept of exploring and embracing autistic identity and culture. You will find a nifty summary of what to expect for each chapter at the very beginning – perfect for those who like to get straight to the point!

At Yellow Ladybugs, we are passionate about amplifying autistic voices, and you'll also find the perspectives of seven well-known Australian and international autistic advocates: JayJay Mudridge, Shadia Hancock, Cherie Clonan, Lauren Melissa Ellzey, Sandhya Menon, Lyric Rivera and Chloe Hayden. We've handpicked these awesome autistic advocates for this book as we recognise they bring tremendous insight into the experiences of autistic girls, women and gender diverse individuals through their work. In mini-interviews found at the end of each chapter, we ask the advocates key questions about what they wish that others under-stood about them, particularly while growing up. We hope you'll draw from their insights, as you support the autistic girls and gender diverse children in your life to embrace their autistic identity and culture and to thrive throughout their life. Throughout the book, you will also find some interesting and thought-provoking quotes from autistic students, parents, teachers and allied health profes-sionals from our Yellow Ladybugs community, who share their lived experience, and guide you with some great advice. Finally, for the dopamine chasers and visual learners, you will also notice some breakout quotes, mantras, and illustrations throughout the book, created by autistic adults, to help bring some key informa-tion and concepts to life.

Do the best
you can
until you
know
better.

MINI INTERVIEW WITH **JAYJAY MUDRIDGE**, NOT ANOTHER AUTISTIC ADVOCATE

Growing up, what do you wish your parent/s had understood about you?

I wish my methods of communication had been listened to. My aggression was never inherent to my autism – it was a sign of my needs not being met – but I was always framed as difficult, aggressive, Too Much. Nobody took the time to understand what my needs were. I also wish they had understood that I heard and understood everything negative they said about me, all of the 'can't dos' and 'nevers' were internalised.

What do you wish your teachers had understood about you?

As a child, I was deemed 'trainable, but not educable', until I wasn't non-speaking anymore. (Around age 12 I had verbal-vocal starved out of me.) I wish they had understood I was reading Proust, reading poetry, not just stimming with the books. But they couldn't conceptualise because I didn't speak. Speaking of stimming, I wish they knew that it helped me process and learn, and if they had just let me do it I likely would have surprised them with my intelligence.

What do you wish your peers had understood about you?

That I'm the shit! I'm truly very cool. Sure, I'll talk about linguistics and poetry more than the average person, but I'm such a consistent, supportive friend and I love being that. I wish they knew about rejection sensitive dysphoria too, that if you don't communicate directly with me my brain starts going haywire, thinking that I'll be rejected and abandoned because I've been rejected and abandoned at every turn. I'm not needy, I just want you to be honest so I can feel safe.

What do you wish you had understood and accepted about yourself?

Had I known about the autistic community, I likely wouldn't have thought of myself as a defective, broken thing. I always knew I was autistic, I just didn't know that neurodiversity is as natural and normal as biodiversity.

What would you like this generation of autistic girls and gender diverse youth to know?

That their unique modalities of existence are not just normal but necessary. That I see poetry in their stims. That the way they communicate is not broken, but beautiful. That my heart sings when I see and hear them self-advocating. That their neurology is the coolest thing there is.

What do you consider to be your autistic strengths?

I care so deeply. I have incredible hyperfocus. My knowledge base is enormous, I have worlds inside of me that I struggle to fit through the tip of my pen. I'm not stubborn; I'm driven. I'm not perseverating; I'm passionate. I see so much beauty in the little things – the sound leaves make when they brush against each other in the wind, the way the sunlight turns green as it sifts through them, the Brownian motion of dust dancing in the air. I'm not in my own world; I'm hyperconnected to this one and it is as beautiful as it is overwhelming.

CHAPTER 1
WHAT'S THE DEAL WITH AUTISM?

CHAPTER HIGHLIGHTS

- **Neuro-affirming language:** Learn all the latest lingo essential to appreciating and respecting the neurodiversity movement. Find out what neuro-affirming care looks and feels like to our community.

- **We value neurodiversity:** There is no right or wrong or broken or perfect. We celebrate all aspects of neurodiversity and neurodivergence.

- **Social model of disability:** We are passionate about promoting the social model of disability. Neurodivergent folks do not need to be 'fixed'. Some neurodivergent people may need extra support or accommodations to live happily and function in a world that is built for the neurotypical majority.

- **Systemic advocacy:** Yellow Ladybugs advocates for systemic change when it comes to improved access to identification, assessment, 'diagnosis' and meaningful supports.

- **Tools and strategies for supporting ladybugs:** Our Yellow Ladybugs community has provided extensive lived experience tips to help support your ladybug.

- **Masking, stimming, meltdowns, shutdowns:** Discussing the importance of some aspects of the autistic identity. These might not ALL be relevant to ALL autistic people.

- **Fight, flight, freeze and fawn:** Understanding common behavioural responses as explained by our community.

A DEFINITION OF AUTISM

So, let's start with a neuro-affirming definition of autism, which, in general, is so poorly understood, with myths and misconceptions abounding. To put it simply, autism is one kind of neurological difference in a neurodiverse world.

---

*'Autism is the lens in which we see, process
and experience the world.
It is a part of who we are.
It is our identity and our culture.'*
– Katie, CEO Yellow Ladybugs

Rather than go down a medical, pathologising description, we hope our shared experiences throughout this book can begin to paint a better picture in your mind of what autism is and isn't. But as an analogy, just like some of us are born left or right-handed, some of us are born autistic (or neurodivergent), and some of us are born neurotypical. Like left-handers, we simply are in the minority. And just like left-handers (who have different writing styles) those of us who are autistic are individual and there is no one autistic way of being. In essence, every autistic human is unique, just as we are all unique human beings.

THE POWER OF LANGUAGE

This is why language is so important for us. The language we use to describe what autism is, holds more power than many realise, and when it is particularly stigmatising and negative, the impacts can run deep, as so eloquently put here by Reframing Autism:

> 'When my child hears such stigmatising language used to describe something that is so integral to their identity, they come to understand their Autism as something that is wrong, an affliction that ideally needs treating in lieu of a cure. They will believe that this thing they have called Autism is wrong and they are inherently disordered. My child is a sensitive soul, so they will internalise this "brokenness" and it will be reinforced each time they encounter this language. My child will come to hate their Autism, and since their Autism is intrinsic to who they are, they will come to hate themselves. They might develop low self-esteem and anxiety, and likely everyone will blame their Autism rather than the language society used to describe it – the language that became my child's inner voice.'

Language has immense power, and how you, your family, teachers and allied health professionals use it, will shape the way your ladybug sees themselves and indeed their world. Speaking of such, let's have a quick look at some of the language and terms you will see throughout this book. If you are familiar with these, feel free to jump ahead.

'Neurodiversity' is commonly an umbrella term used to describe the natural diversity of human brains. 'Neurodivergent' means having a brain that diverges from what is considered typical. Our ladybugs are neurodivergent. You may be neurodivergent if you are autistic, ADHD, dyslexic, have OCD or Bipolar, etc. You are considered 'neurotypical' if your brain does not differ from the norm, or from what society deems as typical. Some of you may be in between, and we colloquially refer to this as 'neuro-questioning' (are they autistic? Am I?). 'Neurodiverse' is the term we use for a group of people with different types of brains. In your family, you may have OCD, your children may be autistic, and your partner may be neurotypical. Together, you are a neurodiverse family. Whereas, if your partner also, say, has dyslexia, you would consider yourselves as a neurodivergent family. We often talk about how difficult it is for those of us in the 'neurominority', living in a world often built by and for the 'neuromajority'. What we are saying here is that the majority of humans are neurotypical, whereas a smaller portion are neurodivergent (the minority).

IS IT A SPECTRUM?

Given the many differences between autistic individuals, autism is sometimes referred to as a spectrum, but there are varying ideas about what the term 'spectrum' actually means. Often, people erroneously think of the autism spectrum as a two-dimensional straight line, with a person with so-called 'severe autism' at one end of the line and one with 'mild autism' at the other. But, as many autists have argued, the linear conception of the autism spectrum is limiting and, ultimately, unfair. It assigns a person to a single, static position, with no room for progress or development, when we know that humans make progress and develop throughout their lives.[2]

To categorise someone as 'high functioning' is often a means of denying support and accommodation; meanwhile, to categorise someone as 'low functioning' ultimately results in low expectations and the denial of support.

Arising from this misleading linear concept of the autism spectrum is an equally misleading series of labels that are commonly used to refer to an autistic person's functioning: references that a person is 'high' or 'low' functioning, that a person's autism is 'mild', 'moderate' or 'severe' or that they are a 'level I', 'II' or 'III'. At Yellow Ladybugs, we cannot emphasise enough that these labels are incredibly dehumanising and can be very damaging to an autistic individual. To categorise someone as 'high functioning' is often a means of denying support and accommodation; meanwhile, to categorise someone as 'low functioning' ultimately results in low expectations and the denial of support. The fact is, any autistic individual's functioning can fluctuate depending on their context and other factors like health, sleep or stress, and the support an individual may require varies across different areas. It is for this reason that you will not encounter any of these terms in this book.

In recent years, there have been numerous attempts to re-envisage the autism spectrum in a more dynamic, multifaceted way, to capture the nuance of autism. We think it is worth taking a moment to review some of these notions to give a clear sense of what we believe the autism spectrum really is.

Rebecca Burgess's comic, 'Understanding the Spectrum', for example, depicts the spectrum as a colour wheel with graded segments representing language, motor skills, perception, executive functioning and sensory filtering.[3]

Another example is 'prism theory', as described by the Chimerical Capuchin.[4] In this conception, the spectrum is explained as light reflected through a prism. Each person has a unique processing prism through which input is filtered and from which light is reflected. That light is the external behaviours that we see. Each person's prism is different, and their prism may change over time as they learn and develop.

Yet another alternative comes from autistic psychologist Rebecca Gannon, who proposes that autism is more like a nebula than a spectrum. Nebulae (those giant spectacular clouds of dust in space) are infinitely dimensional. Expansive. Luminous. All are different. We can't comprehend their existence or scale using 2D or even 3D images. A spectrum, on the other hand, is a linear gradient. Singular. Finite. Thinking of neurodivergence in nebulaic terms makes much more sense. The nebula will be ever-changing and ever-reacting, both from its own internal power and the environment around it – just like autism.

Whichever way you envisage the autism spectrum, it is important to understand it within the context of neurodiversity, as we described earlier, and the undeniable fact that each person's brain is different, and those differences contribute to the rich biodiversity of humans.

TELL ME ABOUT NEURO-AFFIRMING

While we are here, let's quickly introduce some relatively new concepts including 'neuro-affirming' and 'neuro-accessibility'. Neuro-affirming will be different for everyone, which is why we have included a variety of responses from our community on the next page. Hopefully this helps you and your ladybug to begin thinking about and exploring what it means to you also. Neuro-affirming to us means you have considered, acknowledged and validated our autistic identity and culture. It is being mindful of the language you use and appreciating that we want to be the best version of ourselves, not 'neurotypical passing', i.e., a second-rate version of a neurotypical person. It is trying not to change us and make us fit into a version of something that is more socially acceptable to the majority. It is about honouring differences, and not considering them as deficits that need to be fixed. It is not teaching us to suppress who we are, masking our natural selves, so that we can fit in. Neuro-affirming teaching should be all of this and more. Neuro-affirming care and therapy should embrace and understand the Double Empathy Problem[5] and approach any discussion considering all sides, and appreciating and respecting our autistic social communication, sensory and cultural preferences.

For us, it is about adjusting your lens and truly understanding the social model of disability. This means that we are not disabled by our own impairments, but by the failure of our society or external environment to identify and remove any obvious or hidden barriers and properly accommodate our needs.

Our good friend and autistic advocate Annie Crowe further extends neuro-affirming to introduce the concept of neuro-accessibility. For her, neuro-accessibility for students means that the needs of neurodivergent students are specifically considered, and the school environments and services are built or modified so that they can be used by students of all neurotypes. In other words, it is accessible for all neurotypes.

As the term 'neuro-affirming' pops up more and more, we can see that many teachers or allied health professionals are seeking further guidance on how to turn their classroom or practice into a neuro-affirming place. Please be mindful where you seek your training. Many people are now using this as a buzz word, hoping to attract those who are genuinely searching for neuro-affirming practices. We talk more about this in Chapter 3, on school. In the meantime, it is always more beneficial if any training or supports are either neurodivergent led, or at least neurodivergent informed.

NOTES FROM OUR COMMUNITY:
NEURO-AFFIRMING MEANS …

- *Feeling safe to ask for accommodations. – Maddy R*

- *Having my feelings validated and heard. – Debbie B*

- *True freedom to be me. – Chrissy S*

- *Meeting me where I am at, not where society thinks I should be*
  – Jacqui B

- *Socialising how I want and working with the environmental*
  conditions, and adjusting those, not me.
  – Jacqueline L

- *The opportunity for me to be me, and you to be you, and*
  both to be okay and catered for in the best way possible with
  environments so that we can both be us. – Claire E

- *Understanding that we are not trying to 'take advantage'*
  of accommodations that we need. We want to succeed in
  school/work/life, we are not slacking off when we ask for
  accommodations. They are a real and reasonable need.
  – Caroline G

- It looks like listening to people when they tell you something doesn't work for them or suit them, if something is too difficult or stressful. It looks like not assuming I'm not trying hard enough. – *Kitty B*

- Seeing a section for sensory needs on forms, it's having someone announce their willingness to provide inclusive spaces as a given not a gift. It's classrooms where kids can announce their neurodivergence and know that it's welcome. It's public spaces where chill-out zones are included. It's thriving not surviving. Neuro-affirming is soft, gentle, kind, people being welcomed to use their accommodations. It's stimming in public. It's me being supported to thrive as a valued part of society. It's people listening to neurodivergent voices as the primary source for information. It's all the neurodivergent people standing proudly in their identity, showcasing the talents that neurodivergence brings.

- It's living in a household that takes your sensory needs seriously and accommodates them automatically. Without judgement. Mum warning kids before using the vacuum and waiting for them to put on ear defenders before starting. Dad telling everyone to turn volume down and speak one at a time because it's hurting – as soon as they see a wince. It's wearing ear defenders while cooking dinner being completely normal. It's encouraging family members to leave the dinner table after eating for a sensory/people break in their room, even if it's a special occasion. It's asking before going for a hug

and checking the person's skin is covered first. It's modifying
bedrooms when sensory issues are affecting sleep. It's being
able to state you're in sensory overload and ask for rest or
a modified chore list without fearing being called selfish. It's also
coordinating conflicting needs, such as sound sensitivities for
person A who needs to clean the kitchen and person B having
hearing loss who must have the TV volume high. – Lisa A

- *Not feeling pressured to do things outside our comfort zone or*
  being rushed, being able to do things in our own time. Being
  able to use any needed supports without judgement.
  – Leanne O

- *It is having a school recognise adjustments are not 'special*
  treatment' and embracing the need without judgement or issue.
  – Emma

STRENGTHS AND CHALLENGES

Let's turn now to explore what it means to be autistic, including some of the strengths and challenges. Autistic people have many strengths, and it is important to recognise and engage these strengths.

One autistic adult shared with us:

> 'After many years seeing my autism as an embarrassing and shameful thing to hide, I slowly began to realise that I am successful because of my spicy autistic brain, and not in spite of it. I am deeply loyal, passionate, intense and can hyperfocus like no one's business. I own my own business, have a truckload of interests and I'm the person people turn to when they need any problem solved. I am proud of my autistic strengths. I am proud to be autistic.'

Some common autistic strengths our community shared with us include:

- Intense focus
- Strong interests or passions
- A deep connection with animals
- Orthogonal thinking (the ability to think laterally)
- Pattern recognition
- Good memory

- Highly receptive to sensory input
- Honesty
- Deep empathy

Your ladybug may take years to identify their strengths, passions and interests. In the meantime consider autistic role models (we talk about that in Chapter 6) and have a look out for Chloe Hayden's videos on finding your eye sparkle.

IT'S NOT ALL SUNSHINE AND RAINBOWS

Like everyone, autistic people face challenges too, often arising from the fact that the world is set up for a non-autistic majority. Equally important as recognising and engaging autistic strengths is identifying and supporting our challenges, and looking at the unmet needs we have as individuals. Some of the challenges that autistic people may face include:

- Sensory processing differences leading to overload
- Social and communication styles that differ from the neuromajority
- Finding transitions or changes stressful
- Bullying and exclusion
- Executive functioning
- Rejection sensitivity
- Anxiety

We will go into these things in more detail in the following chapters.

AUTISM PREVALENCE

So just how common is autism?

How many of you have heard that frustrating saying 'In my day, we never had all this "autism" stuff'. Oh, the comebacks that could be said, often thought of late at night, with the strong sense of 'argh, I should have said that'. Yes, we are seeing more autistic people being identified. In fact, studies are now saying it is something like 1 in 44 children, an increase from previous years of 1 in 68 in 2021 and 1 in 150 in 2000. By the way, our comeback to those who say 'in my day' is usually that in your day, we failed generations of children and adults, who were just labelled as troublemakers, naughty, lazy and hopeless. That usually keeps them quiet. And in truth, it doesn't really matter what percentage of us are autistic, the important thing is that we are slowly getting better at identifying autism. However, we still have a long way to go in identifying autistic females, and those individuals of all genders who don't present in a stereotypical way.

Now let's add gender into the mix. Over recent years, the most commonly quoted studies suggest that boys are four times more likely to receive an autism diagnosis than girls. So, what does this tell us? There is certainly a prominent gender difference in official diagnosis rates[6] and perhaps the issue is that these diagnostic rates do not accurately capture the actual prevalence of autism across all genders. Instead, they point to a diagnostic bias, which leads to girls often being underdiagnosed.

*'No one believed my daughter was autistic.
I was turned away time and time again.
They told me that she has friends, can make
eye contact and greeted the paediatrician
at the door. She was failed miserably by a
system that isn't catching up quick enough
to what we know – girls can be autistic too!'*
– Natalia, autistic parent

WHAT RESEARCH TELLS US

Many researchers are now exploring why the diagnostic process is less likely to favour girls.[7] One of the key reasons is that the assessment tools used for diagnosis and research in the field of autism have almost always been developed from research focused on boys.[8] In other words, there is an established gender bias, both in the diagnostic tools, and in the field of autism research.

The most recent research is beginning to confirm what the autistic community has long suspected, which is that there are as many autistic females as there are males. A June 2022 study found that when the common clinical tools are adjusted for sex biases, roughly the same percentage of boys and girls are identified as autistic.[9] We note here too, that studies are yet to accurately account for the gender diverse autistic population, many of whom are being missed for the same reasons that women and girls are missed.

THE IMPACT

The implications of this discrepancy are significant, as a result many autistic girls, women and gender diverse people continue to be misunderstood, misdiagnosed or missed altogether. We have become known as the 'lost generation' – always here, but unseen and often not even being looked for.

An autistic adult recently shared their experiences growing up as a lost girl:

> *'I've been working my entire life to blend in, never feeling quite at home. The signs were all there. But they were always missed. I never fit in. I was always on the outside watching in. Why didn't they like me? What was wrong with me? Being an outsider, ignored and forgotten about, it all made me feel so lost. Lost about who I was, what I needed and where I was going. What a relief to finally find myself through autism. There was nothing wrong with me. I was not broken, no less, I was just different to them.'*

In addition to the discrepancies in diagnosis rates, it also takes two to three years longer, on average, for girls to be diagnosed compared to their male peers.[10] One recent study estimates that 80 per cent of autistic females remain undiagnosed or misdiagnosed at the age of 18.[11] While boys are often diagnosed in their early childhood years, for girls, the average age of diagnosis is nine years.[12] The impact of a later autism diagnosis being made can be enormous. By nine, an autistic girl (or gender diverse individual) has already navigated crucial life stages, including early childhood, the transition to school and friendships, often without appropriate support or understanding from their family, caregivers and educators. And you can imagine the impact of an even later diagnosis – well into a girl or gender diverse individual's teenage years or even adulthood. So, to summarise: autistic girls, women and gender diverse individuals seem to be overlooked due to four key factors:

- Autistic girls, women and gender diverse individuals presenting differently
- Gender bias in screening tools and diagnostic criteria
- Existing stereotypes about how autism presents
- Lack of clinicians' training and experience in recognising autism in girls

'We have been overlooked for many reasons including prevailing stereotypes of what autism looks like, the gender bias of standard diagnostic tools, and the way girls are socialised and viewed in our society. More generally, we know that many autistic girls, women and gender diverse individuals are being missed, or having their needs invalidated because of their more hidden or internalised autistic presentation.'
– Katie Koullas, CEO, Yellow Ladybugs

MASKING

Camouflaging, or masking, is the attempt to cover up difficulties in social settings. Most people make minor adjustments to their behaviour to fit in socially, but camouflaging or masking requires a constant focus. It is widely recognised that girls and gender diverse individuals are good at masking their autistic traits to fit in with their peers. Some examples include suppressing repetitive behaviours, stims or discussion of their intense interests, pretending to follow a conversation they don't understand, or imitating the behaviour of those around them. (It is worth noting that some autistic males can and do mask, but they do so not nearly as commonly as females.)

'When I am able to mask, I may make it through an hour, but invariably, my mask soon slips and like Cinderella at the ball, I am left escaping in tears for fear of the "real me" being exposed.' – Chantell, @shylittlepixie

Autistic masking looks different for every autistic individual. It is complex, and can be a burden, a necessity and a privilege. Masking may help an autistic person to blend in socially, often well into their adult life, forging relationships and advancing careers, but the burden comes though and with it the high price of exhaustion and anxiety, which often lead to poor mental health.

It is well known that repetitive behaviours in autism serve a vital role in emotional regulation, and the impact of suppressing stims over extended periods while masking can be great. Many autistic adults who have spent a significant portion of their life masking also report a sense of loss of identity and alienation. Masking may also be a necessity for some, especially our BIPOC and CALD autistic community, who may find it unsafe to navigate an unjust society as an unmasked autistic person.

An important point about masking is that it is not always a conscious thing, and it can take an autistic person years of reflection on their behaviour to figure out their 'mask' and learn how to act without it. From our lived experience, the consensus is that many of us feel like we have been living our lives according to other people's expectations. This is why it is so important for your ladybug to understand what masking and unmasking might look like.

One autistic adult shared this with us:

'It just didn't feel safe to be me. I was just too different. The only way I knew how to cope with that pain was to watch from the sidelines. It felt safe there, almost like I was undercover, and I could do my best detective work trying to figure out who I could talk, dress and be like, so I would get their elusive approval. I studied them, practised their mannerisms, but it was a lot of work. It was exhausting, and caused such intense anxiety, leading me to withdraw, retreat and hide away again.'

THE HIDDEN PRESENTATION

So, how can one spot this hidden presentation, commonly seen in autistic girls and gender diverse individuals? We are trying to move away from 'lists' and prescriptive notions on what autism is and isn't. We would prefer you learn about what it means to be an autistic girl or gender diverse young person through our stories and reflections. This is why we have included so many thoughtful commentaries from our neurokin throughout the book. It will give you a better idea of the fascinating, complex, truly wonderful way we can think, feel, sense, perceive and connect with the world around us. However, we have curated below some common traits you may see in our ladybugs and those who are high-maskers. Many of us (but not all of us) may:

- Immerse ourselves in deep focus on passions of a particular subject or interest
- Have a preference for a small social circle, usually one to two safe friends
- Show strong leadership in play with peers (seen as controlling by others) and lean towards less reciprocal play
- Be selective with whom we communicate (seen as 'very shy')
- Be less prone to following traditional social conventions
- Be high maskers, for example, withhold anxiety in public then melt down or shut down once at home
- Be interested in socialising but unsure how to approach making connections
- Have sensory sensitivities

- Feel emotions intensely and display extreme reactions to what others 'perceive' as minor problems
- Interpret language literally
- Be more fluid in gender identity and expression
- Be extremely empathetic, nurturing and sensitive
- Have great attention to detail, noticing many things others miss
- Have an incredible imagination
- Be a perfectionist in some areas and at the same time find basic routine tasks overwhelming
- Prefer playing with boys in physical activities rather than engaging in small talk with girls[13]

Please remember that we are all unique and individual, and whilst this list has been developed through our collective lived experience, it does not replace any official diagnostic criteria, which as side note, is extremely pathologising and turns our differences into disorders.

There are a number of misconceptions that arise due to our high masking and this 'hidden' or more internalised presentation. Some girls and gender diverse individuals are dismissed as autistic and as we described above, deemed to be 'just a little shy'. Alternatively, our ladybugs might be thought of as 'very social', when in fact masking is in full play, with great effort made to mimic and fit in. Also, some of us will move between groups of children, creating this appearance, but we may not be developing or have the opportunity to develop deep connections.

One young autistic adult shared:

> *'I was a high masker. I felt like an alien, faking it to fit in at school. I would move from social group to social group throughout high school because I could not find a place to fit in. I would blend in for a while but end up being overwhelmed and tired from trying to be someone I was not. And often, when I did try and embrace and embody my authentic self, I was either actually rejected or I sabotaged things because I would assume I was being rejected from my classmates.'*

Another misconception is that our ladybugs do not have any repetitive behaviours or 'obscure' interests – one of the requirements in the diagnosis manual. Let's consider that maybe our preference for repetition may be just more subtle and more socially accepted. For example, we may fidget, twirl our hair or bite our nails, suppressing more obvious and less socially accepted displays such as flapping or spinning. Our ladybugs' interests may be just as intense as those of their male counterparts, but they may entail more socially accepted subjects, such as animals, music or celebrities – interests that closely resemble those of her typical peers.

'Mum, how do people make friends?
I don't get it ...'

It is therefore no great surprise that the journey to 'diagnosis' is often long and fraught, with both a lack of expertise and recognition. Parents' concerns are regularly dismissed by health professionals who infer that the girl or gender diverse child is 'just shy', 'just anxious', 'just a little depressed' – or even that there is a parenting problem. We have heard that many parents find themselves visiting psychologist after psychologist, paediatrician after paediatrician, as they attempt to uncover their child's neurology and find ways to support them.

One parent shared this story with us:

'Our daughter has recently had her autism professionally validated in Grade 4 – which I know is still quite young compared to other stories we have heard. It is frustrating though, because we were dismissed for so long. As a younger child, she always presented with extreme anxiety, sensory challenges and can be socially awkward at times (like her mumma) but is witty, kind and intensely observant when with her limited inner circle of trusted connections. At school in her younger years, she was very compliant although often had trouble speaking in class, but no concerns were ever raised. Over the years we mentioned a few times that she might need some support building confidence and friendships as she was lonely, and she often found school distressing when the environment got loud and busy or was unpredictable. Those requests were largely dismissed as teachers are completely overloaded most of the time and she was observed to be fine, despite her telling us how lonely she

was at school. We tried to offer her guidance as parents but it's really impossible not being at school. More recently in Grade 5, as we drove home, she asked me point blank, "Mum, how do people make friends? I don't get it …" What an amazing insight into her way of thinking. What she needed was a low-pressure discussion with a trusted person about how she might know if people want to be her friend, about how she might engage on a special interest with likeminded peers, how she might be able to join an activity at lunchtime if she was supported to do so. Although it's great we are building supports for her now slowly, it is a heavy reminder that she has already completed most of her primary years. We hope for other ladybugs that through advocacy and ongoing education we can build knowledge around identification and supports for autistic girls and gender diverse students to ensure they are supported much earlier in their schooling journey.'

THE DIAGNOSIS OR 'IDENTIFICATION' JOURNEY

If you have already had your ladybug formally identified as autistic, you are welcome to jump ahead further in this chapter, or feel free to stay as we explore this topic. We will use the terms 'diagnosed' and 'identified' interchangeably here. Whilst we have a strong preference towards 'identified' (autism is not a disease or illness to be diagnosed), we will also use the terms diagnosed and diagnosis for now. This is to help those who are new to this concept, or only familiar with the medically driven process of being assessed for autism, which is unfortunately the only pathway there is if you are exploring formal recognition or confirmation that your child is autistic.

DO YOU NEED TO GET A FORMAL 'DIAGNOSIS'?

As adults we always say self-identification is valid. However, for children, we want to acknowledge that it is harder to get services, adjustments and accommodations without an official 'diagnosis'. At school, many of our ladybugs are refused adjustments without a formal diagnosis, and even once they do have one, the frustration continues because they are often seen as not disruptive enough to warrant tailored supports. For those in Australia, the only way to get meaningful funded supports outside of school is through our NDIS system. Many of our ladybugs miss out on this, as they are deemed 'not autistic enough' or 'high functioning' which, as we described earlier, totally dismisses the often hidden and internalised needs.

We talk about this in our school chapter (Chapter 3), but it is worth repeating here that there are many barriers to seeking a formal autism diagnosis. We want to acknowledge the families who might have other intersectional barriers to diagnosis including those of lower socio-economic status or our BIPOC and CALD communities who might not always have the access to appropriate resources to seek out an assessment. We acknowledge this is a failing of our system, and we continue to highlight this issue in the hope of creating systemic change.

GOING FOR IT

So, you might decide to bite the bullet and go for the assessment. Firstly, begin saving. It's ridiculously expensive, and it really shouldn't be. Secondly, we do want to let you know that it can be hard to remain positive and neuro-affirming when getting our young people formally diagnosed, given that the whole process of getting assessed and diagnosed is deficit-based, pathologising and not at all focused on our autistic strengths. Autism is a neurology, not a disease; it is not a disorder, and yet this is where the diagnosis experience takes us. The medical model that the assessment process adheres to is vastly unhelpful and so stigmatising. Many members of our community have described this process as traumatising and stressful. So, when you do choose to explore a diagnosis, it is really important to try and find a team who are safe, and who choose language that is more aligned to the social model of disability.

One parent shared their frustration with the system.

'I am a single mum, on a fixed income. This entire process has been woeful and exhausting. It feels like one hurdle after the other. There was a 12-month wait list just to begin the process, and that was with our local paediatrician. They dismissed us instantly, so we jumped online and luckily I found someone to recommend a psychologist familiar with autistic girls. The trouble was that there was another 12-month wait list, and we lived regionally, so we had to travel quite the distance for every appointment. So much wasted time. It also cost thousands of dollars I didn't have, which nearly ruined me financially and emotionally, but it was such a relief to finally find someone who got her straightaway. It was a world of difference.'

THE AUTISTIC EXPERIENCE

We now want to turn to some of the key aspects of the autistic experience that you will need to understand as you make your way through this book. The following list is by no means exhaustive, but simply provides some background that will be useful as you read on. We hope that through greater understanding, you will find the confidence to begin to question things and seek the support you and your family need.

SENSORY PROCESSING

One of the hallmark characteristics of autism is sensory processing differences. These differences are a fundamental part of a person's way of experiencing the world. While every human has their own unique sensory profile, for those with sensory processing differences, their sensory needs and preferences will likely be much more significant than most other people and affect their lives in many ways. It can be difficult for non-autistic people to appreciate how these differences can make life both challenging and wonderful.

There are two types of sensory processing differences: hypersensitivity and hyposensitivity. Someone who is *hypersensitive* tends to be defensive or avoidant of sensory input, that is, sights, sounds, smells, tastes or touch. A person who is hypersensitive tends to find certain sensory input disturbing, even though such input is not disturbing to most other people around them. For example, a visit to a large shopping centre is unlikely to be greatly bothersome to the average, neurotypical person. But for a hypersensitive autistic person, it can be overwhelming, with lots of noises from crowds and music as well as a range of different lighting. Add to this a trip to the toilets with unpleasant smells and noisy hand dryers, and for a hypersensitive person you have a recipe for sensory overload.

'Sensory seeking is a form of self-regulation, where we seek stimulation and sensory input. We should never stop someone seeking this out.' – *Sonny Jane Wise*

Someone who is *hyposensitive* to sensory stimuli tends to seek out certain sights, sounds, smells, tastes or touch, and will crave that sensory input much more than most other people around them. For example, in the case of someone who is auditory hyposensitive, they may play music or television loudly, they may make a lot of noise generally and may seem oblivious to certain verbal cues or other sounds. It's important to note that you can be hyposensitive with some senses and hypersensitive to others, and these can shift and change depending on a variety of reasons.

One autistic parent shared their experience with sensory processing.

'It took me a long time to understand what my own sensory profile was, well into my 40s. It wasn't until my child began exploring theirs, that we both sat down to discuss what we found stimulating (sensory seeking) and what caused us distress (sensory avoiding). What is really interesting is that we are complete opposites, and this explains why we sometimes have so many situations where we are both overwhelmed and not tuned into each other's needs. We are getting better at understanding them, and being able to work out a strategy that helps us both feel connected and regulated.'

VESTIBULAR, PROPRIOCEPTION AND INTEROCEPTION, OH MY!

Along with the more common senses of taste, touch, smell, sight, and hearing, three other senses are important to consider: vestibular, proprioception and interoception. Vestibular is concerned with balance, while proprioception is the ability to sense where your body is in space. For example, many people with differences in proprioception trip over things and bump into things a lot. Both vestibular and proprioception can result in challenges with gross motor activities, such as riding a bicycle. Interoception is the awareness of our internal body sensations, for example, knowing when we are hungry or too hot. Someone who experiences interoceptive hypersensitivity may be hyperaware of their body's signals, often feeling sick or unwell. Alternatively, someone who experiences interoceptive hyposensitivity may struggle with toileting, forget to eat or drink for long periods or may not register pain signals. Interoception is also linked to our internal awareness of our emotional state, i.e., knowing how we 'feel'.

It is important to keep in mind that your ladybug is not going to experience every sensory stimulus in a certain way all the time. Sensory needs and preferences can change from day to day and over time. Sensory sensitivities are often increased at times of greater arousal, such as during periods of heightened anxiety. Also, those with sensory processing differences might have a mixed profile and be hypersensitive in some areas and hyposensitive in others.

Sensory regulation refers to our ability to change to reduce sensory overload. It is our brain's ability to calm down or become more alert depending on the environment. It can take quite some time to uncover a person's sensory needs and preferences. You may find occupational therapy useful in helping to understand your autistic child's sensory profile and to support their sensory processing differences.

There are a range of tools and strategies which can help aid sensory regulation. Some examples include:

- Fidget toys
- Sunglasses, hoodies and light covers in areas of bright lighting
- Noise-cancelling headphones
- Choosing soft, loose or otherwise comfortable clothing
- Planning to ensure that exposure to stimuli is reduced
- Weighted blankets or cushions

Finally, it is worth noting that although sensory processing differences may cause a person discomfort or overwhelm them, these can greatly enhance a person's experience of the world. Some people with sensory processing differences may find their heightened senses useful to them in everyday life as they notice sensory stimuli that others may not notice at all. Sometimes heightened sensory perception can even bring a sense of wonder and joy – for example, a person who immerses themselves in nature and the remarkable sights, sounds, smells, tastes and textures around them.

One teen ladybug shared:

> 'ASMR videos make me feel so happy. Whenever the world feels too much and I need to ground myself, I jump on YouTube for Kids and watch videos of people poking slime or cutting into soap. It's such a wave of relaxation and joy.'

STIMMING

Stimming, a shortened form of the pathologised term 'self-stimulatory behaviour', involves repetitive body movements. Just as every human has their own sensory profile, every human stims – examples are nail biting, skin picking or hair twirling. But autistic people tend to stim a lot more than non-autistic people because of their sensory differences.

Stimming serves a whole bunch of purposes. It can help to regulate one's emotions, to manage anxiety, to amuse oneself and even to express one's emotions. Stimming is a form of body language, and it is just as valid a form of self-expression and communication as neurotypical body language. Accepting your autistic child's stimming – their natural autistic body language – is one way you can demonstrate an understanding of your child's needs and autistic identity.

OVERLOAD

Our ladybugs can experience overload and be overwhelmed, which can be described as a feeling that our brain is 'full'. There are several ways in which we can experience overload. This is a completely normal experience for autistic people and should not be punished or criticised. Rather, an understanding of the causes and triggers can be helpful for parents, caregivers and educators – and for the autistic person, too.

We all experience different stressors in our lives. For most neurotypical people these come and go and do not reach a level or threshold where there is overload (stress threshold). For neurotypical people, these ups and downs often don't reach the threshold where significant overload occurs. For neurodivergent individuals, the baseline level sits at a higher level to begin with. This means that on a day-to-day basis, neurodivergent individuals are operating at levels closer to the stress threshold. In addition to this, the peaks and troughs are often steeper as well. This means we can experience a greater stress response from a given situation.

So, while the usual daily stressors that a neurotypical person may experience cause no real trauma or stress response, for us, these same experiences can lead to meltdowns and shutdowns.

These responses or 'behaviours', as they are often called by health and education professionals, are the symptom of the overload. They are not conscious behaviours we choose.

MELTDOWNS

Meltdowns are one of the most misunderstood aspects of our experience. One of the most important things for parents, caregivers and educators to understand about a meltdown, is that this is not 'bad behaviour' or 'being naughty', or attention seeking. The more meltdowns we go through with our young people, the better we become at anticipating them and understanding the triggers. Time and space are usually the first step for a loved one who is experiencing a meltdown.

Meltdowns can also occur because of environments that are over-stimulating. One of the challenges for autistic people is understanding what things in our environment cause this, and then finding ways to reduce excessive sensory input. For example, some people find wearing sunglasses indoors helpful. Noise-cancelling headphones and avoiding busy places at peak times can also be useful.

Meltdowns can also result from the compacting stress of lots of social situations in a short timeframe and the need to mask and appear 'okay'. Meltdowns can also occur sometime after the initial trigger, as masking may be used to 'survive' the situation until a safe environment can be sought.

It is also important to consider that meltdowns may look very different for different people. The signs of a meltdown can include increased stimming or fidgeting, crying, shouting, hyperventilating, an inability to communicate, head hitting and kicking.

Being aware of the possibility of a meltdown can help parents plan outings. Often having a backup plan or an exit plan is critical. Frequently asking ourselves, *is this essential?* and *why is this a rule?* can help to negotiate the neurotypical world of expectations and how they impact our autistic young people.

One parent shared their journey from a 'tough love' approach to a more understanding one:

> *'I had to shift my thinking and learn how to respond empathetically to my child's meltdowns. What I was doing wasn't working and made things much worse. Once I opened my eyes to what I was doing, I felt a crushing and intense amount of guilt. I thought I was helping them in the long term, I was invisible to the trauma I was causing. As soon as I reframed my thinking, and learned their behaviour is involuntary, and just a distressed response to their overwhelm, I was able to connect more with love and empathy. This changed everything.'*

I deserve to be gentle and understanding with myself.

SHUTDOWNS

You might find the terms 'meltdown' and 'shutdown' used inter-changeably; however, the two are quite different. Shutdowns occur when someone either completely, or in some part, withdraws. This might be to a safe place, such as a sensory space or bedroom, or by becoming silent and not communicating. A shutdown can also be experienced as appearing to be frozen or not being able to move or communicate.

Sometimes people consider a shutdown as an inward response, and a meltdown as an outward response. But it's not quite so clean cut and simple. These responses are due to overload breaching our stress threshold. This could be due to things like unexpected changes in plans, sensory overload or internal triggers including feelings of shame or inadequacy from ongoing negative self-talk. Other triggers can include being rushed with decisions or being asked to provide an explanation for something without time to prepare a response.

It can be hard for parents who have always cuddled and comforted their upset child in the past to now face what appears as rejection of this comfort. This is not personal, but rather a reflection of the need for quiet and a low-sensory environment with few demands.

How can you help your autistic young person in a shutdown? Providing space is an absolute necessity. Bring food and water, but don't be offended if it is refused. Don't expect usual routines and activities to be followed. Personal hygiene and other activities may be a low priority as their brains need time to rest and recover. Even though as parents we may want to hug or physically comfort our child, this may cause additional sensory overload. Always ask permission. It can be hard for parents who have always cuddled and comforted their upset child in the past to now face what appears as rejection of this comfort. This is not personal, but rather a reflection of the need for quiet and a low-sensory environment with few demands.

As parents, caregivers and educators, we can encourage our autistic girls and gender diverse young people to ask for space and breaks, and respect requests for these. If you sense that a meltdown or shutdown may be looming, you can offer support by providing space and breaks that are guilt free for your young person.

With so many changes happening in the tween and teen years, there are going to be many triggers experienced both internally and externally for our ladybugs. Having an awareness of the triggers and responding with care, support and no judgement, are key to providing the safety and support needed.

FLIGHT, FIGHT, FREEZE AND FAWN

Our autonomic nervous system is responsible for controlling many unconscious vital functions like breathing and digestion. This system is also responsible for our body's perception and unconscious response to threats and danger – think of it like a crisis control centre. Polyvagal theory, developed by Dr Stephen Porges, has been referred to as the science of safety and offers some scientific explanations of how our body responds to threats. The autonomic nervous system, or our crisis control centre, is comprised of the sympathetic and the parasympathetic nervous systems. These systems are generally both active and work together to keep balance.

Most of us are familiar with two of the common stress responses – fight and flight. These are the need to either run away from danger or to face up to and tackle danger, and are sometimes referred to as the 'I can' responses. Flight comes as panic, fear, anxiety and the need to run, while fight can often be experienced as rage, anger and frustration. These are responses by our sympathetic nervous system, and we can experience symptoms such as increased heart rate, breathing and release of stored energy.

While we may be familiar with fight and flight, there are two less familiar but equally important stress responses: freeze and fawn (fawn is also sometimes known as appease). These responses are driven by our parasympathetic nervous system, which is concerned with conserving energy and increasing digestion.

Freeze is when the body is unable to move or act against a threat and is often referred to as an 'I can't' response. You might experience a sense of dread, feeling numb and a decreasing heart rate. Freeze can be associated with feelings of shame, hopelessness and being trapped.

Fawn is a response where someone wants to please others and is overly agreeable or helpful to avoid conflict. A fawning individual will often say yes to requests to avoid conflict even when they know they are unable to meet the request. Autistic people can feel safer meeting others' needs rather than their own. This might be a type of masking; we help others and support everyone while ignoring our own needs and we don't let people know what we need. Unfortunately, this instinct can also make us vulnerable to exploitation, manipulation and abuse. You can read more about this in Chapter 5, on healthy relationships, gender and sexuality.

An autistic adult in our community reflected on their experience of fawning:

'I have always been a people pleaser, well before I knew what the term fawning meant. I now refer to myself as a recovering fawner. The cost of doing it got too high. I hated confrontation of any kind, so I would agree with anything, unable to voice any form of disagreement. It started in childhood and followed me throughout my life. It was my survival instincts kicking in, not ever wanting to be different and always wanting to appease.'

Understanding these non-voluntary responses to increasing stress is crucial to supporting our ladybugs, and indeed our own way of experiencing the world.

Illustration: Em Hammond/Neurowild

REJECTION SENSITIVITY

RSD (Rejection Sensitivity Dysphoria) is an extreme emotional response to the perception that we have failed, or even the fear of failure. The reaction can be so severe it triggers feelings of worthlessness and pain. Rather than give textbook definitions on what rejection sensitivity is, we prefer to share what it feels like, to help paint the picture for you.

One autistic adult shared:

> 'Rejection sensitivity frames my whole life, personally and professionally. It feels like you will be rejected all the time, whether it's perceived rejection or real rejection. And this can impact our relationships because we are anticipating this rejection. Even if we haven't experienced any form of rejection, it comes from the trauma of growing up and how our brains are wired. We often read a lot into certain things and it can be really exhausting. It's more than a typical rejection feeling, it affects all parts of your body and mind and soul.'

Another good illustration is this quote shared with us from an autistic student:

> 'It didn't really matter what it was, a harsh comment, slight criticism or even just a change in someone's tone of voice, it all made me feel the same way. Like I had done something terrible, and everyone around me knew it. My face would heat up and

I'd fight back tears, wishing more than anything to be invisible. I would feel this way for hours, unable to think or feel anything other than immense, overwhelming shame.'

This insightful experience from a now adult ladybug shows how little rejection sensitivity is understood, and how big the impact is. So, what are the unmet needs here? She continued:

'Understanding and reassurance would have been a big help. I was such a people pleaser, the thought of ever doing something "wrong" was a huge trigger. I would SOMETIMES have teachers notice after a certain comment that I would withdraw and can remember only one teacher ever checking in with me and saying "I'm sorry if I upset you with what I said earlier. You're doing a really good job, but I just needed you to ..." and then finishing with another reassurance. If only they looked deeper. I now know that I also needed safety. If something had to be said, I needed it to be done in private, after class when no one was around. The hardest thing for me was if anything was said to me in front of other students and feeling exposed on top of the shame. People always said to me "no one is going to remember it, or never think about it again" but for me, if I've also been exposed, it feels like they'll be judging me for eternity.'

COMEBACKS

Before we move onto our next chapter, we wanted to add a tip for those of us who will undoubtably come across so many ignorant, ableist and hurtful comments. By the way, at its heart, ableism is rooted in the assumption that disabled people require 'fixing' and is the discrimination and social prejudice against people with disabilities. We hate ableism, and whilst it is always a good feeling when we can advocate for ourselves and our loved ones, we don't always have to join every conversation we have been invited to. With limited energy, spoons (google spoon theory) and time, please pick your battles, conserve your energy and remember you do not owe anyone your time or education. It's your choice.

We have started by introducing some of the challenges of being autistic, but there is so much to be celebrated when you embrace autistic culture and identity – as will be shown in the remaining chapters of the book. We will be learning from lived autistic experience which, as we know, is the most powerful way we can learn to support and advocate for our ladybugs.

MINI INTERVIEW:
SHADIA HANCOCK,
AUTISM ACTUALLY

Growing up, what do you wish your parent/s had understood about you?

The biggest thing I want to emphasise to parents is that it can be easy to become overwhelmed with different viewpoints when discovering a family member is autistic. When I was young, deficits-based perspectives regarding autism were common-place, with the majority of discussion around autism being led by non-autistic professionals. My family's introduction to autism was being handed a wad of papers with a checklist.

I would encourage parents to seek out the voices of autistic adults, parents, and autistic speech pathologists, psychologists, and other professionals as hearing autistic adults' insights gave my parents a greater understanding of what I may have been experiencing as a child. It can also be difficult to think about the future, but I would urge parents to try and focus on what we are achieving right now, and where we are developmentally. Autism is not a doom-and-gloom diagnosis.

What do you wish your teachers had understood about you?

As a high-masking student, many of my challenges in the classroom went unnoticed. My anxiety is constant; however, my oftentimes neutral facial expression doesn't indicate that anything is wrong. I also tend to laugh when I am distressed; to neurotypicals, this may indicate that I am happy, when I am actually experiencing the opposite. I felt like the only times my disability was 'seen' was when I would have a panic attack or meltdown. Many people remark to me that I don't 'look' autistic (whatever that means). I think it is important when working with any autistic student to remember that what we are going through internally does not always externalise. Before jumping to conclusions about our 'behaviours' and labelling them as naughty, manipulative and the like, I would urge you to consider our individual strengths, challenges and possible triggers in the environment. Be our biggest ally by looking beyond our behaviours and considering why we may have acted in a certain way.

What do you wish your peers had understood about you?

Disclosure has been really helpful when working with peers and making friends, as it gives them context as to why I may socialise and interact differently to others, and when I may need further clarification. My method of communication is very blunt, and I do not understand hidden meanings behind requests that are made to me, which probably contributed to me being ostracised and misunderstood throughout primary and high school. For example, when my peers asked me to give feedback on their work, I followed their requests by listing the positives, and what needed to be improved. I would then get puzzled when I would receive the silent treatment, and it took me many years to realise that they were only looking for particular kinds of feedback. Now I am able to say to people, 'I am very honest and blunt as I am autistic. Let me know if you would like feedback', so they are not offended if I say something that is perhaps too honest. I also wish that my peers had known more about diversity in general, and why I didn't like going to parties or socialising after school. If my peers had realised that going to loud and bright events with strangers was anxiety-inducing and overwhelming my senses, they may have tried to include me in more autism-friendly settings rather than me just being excluded.

> *'If my peers had realised that going to loud and bright events with strangers was anxiety-inducing and overwhelming my senses, they may have tried to include me in more autism-friendly settings rather than me just being excluded.'*

What do you wish you had understood and accepted about yourself?

I wish I could tell my 13-year-old self that being autistic is a difference to be embraced and celebrated, not something to feel ashamed about. I would tell myself that the reason why people bullied me was not because I am abnormal or not good enough; it is a problem with the other person. Finally, I wish I could tell my younger self that accepting my challenges is an important part of developing a positive autistic identity, and that it is okay to ask for help. I do not need to compare my self-worth and achievements to peers and neurotypicals; I am enough as myself.

What would you like this generation of autistic girls and gender diverse youth to know?

I hope that younger autistic individuals know that diversity in all forms is an important aspect of society; if we didn't have different thinkers, the world would be quite boring! When I was younger, I thought I would never find people I related to and could resonate with – now, with so many autistic role models from a variety of backgrounds, cultural identities, gender and sexual identities, and support needs, I have amazing connections and no longer feel isolated. While it may seem like you are all alone, it is reassuring to know that there are people who share your neurology out there. Another thing I would like to emphasise is that autism is an identity and a different way of communicating, perceiving and interacting with the world; it is not disordered, deficient or abnormal!

What do you consider to be your autistic strengths?

My attention to detail allows me to notice things others may not. It also gives me strengths with analysing and interpreting information. I feel this has helped me with my drawing skills as I am able to sense when aspects of a composition seem inaccurate and work on particular elements in isolation. I am also highly attuned to other people's emotional states; while this can cause difficulties with humans, it has been helpful in connecting with animals as they too are very sensitive to the emotional states of others. Animals communicate in ways other than spoken language, and I feel I can interpret their body language and communication far easier than humans. I love the way I can immerse myself in my passions and become an expert in my areas of interest; this has influenced my career path and my friendship circles. I feel I have a strong sense of justice, which has influenced my interest in autism advocacy and other extracurricular interests like climate change, animal welfare and sustainability.

CHAPTER 2
HOME LIFE
– PACE YOURSELF

CHAPTER HIGHLIGHTS

- **Autistic-approved strategies to support complex behaviour:**
There can be a lot of noise around therapy and support strategies.
We believe it is best to prioritise autistic-approved strategies.
We focus on co-regulation and the PACE strategy (Playfulness
Acceptance Curiosity and Empathy).

- **Creating a safe, autistic-affirming home environment:** This is the
gift of empowering your ladybug to better understand themselves,
to feel accepted and to identify all the positive aspects of being
autistic. Peer support networks like Yellow Ladybugs promote peer
connection and help to build supportive communities.

- **Understanding differences in autistic communication:** We know
that communication styles can be quite different for neurodivergent
people compared to the neurotypical majority. Being aware of
differences and preferences can help build understanding. We focus
on stimming, fidgeting, language and literal thinking.

- **Minimising overwhelm at home:** Most likely your home is a safe
space for your ladybug. We offer some ideas around making your
home more sensory and autistic-friendly, and say why it is important.

- **Family dynamics:** Getting into the nitty gritty when it comes to
living in a complex family unit. All the relationships within a home
includes parenting, those co-parenting, sibling relationships and
extended family and friends. Identifying areas where you might be
able to reduce triggers and stressors is important.

- **Unsolicited advice is a big no thanks:** Why unsolicited advice is
unhelpful. Lived experience tips on how you might start setting up
some boundaries for you and your family.

For many ladybugs, home is often their safe place. In fact, let's narrow that down and say their bedroom may feel like their only sanctuary. This is especially true, leading up to and during their teen years. It is the place where, after a day full of masking, sensory overwhelm, navigating social expectations, learning or just living in a world not built for them, they can relax and be themselves. It is also a space they can retreat to, especially when there are complex family dynamics at play, competing needs with siblings or even sensory triggers from other family members. Home can also be where you get to see your ladybug shine their brightest, and where you can exhale yourself – letting go of all social judgements and expectations. On the flip side, home can be a stark reminder of the isolation you feel as a neurodiverse (or perhaps neurodivergent) family, and how unsupportive and inaccessible the world can be. This can not only be hard on your children, but it can also be hard for you too. Sometimes, trying to create a safe and peaceful home environment can feel like trying to catch lightning in a bottle: meaning, it seems impossible or at best rare. But together, we can explore ways that might make it easier for you and your family.

In this chapter, we will explore some of these challenges that occur within the home, including understanding behaviours, along with some of the Yellow Ladybugs-approved strategies that you can use to support your young one when they are struggling. Drawing from our own experiences, we will then look into other autistic-approved recommendations that can help your child feel safe and supported within your home environment, including topics such as accepting their autistic identity, understanding autistic communication and ways to help minimise sensory overwhelm. We will conclude with looking into some of the dynamics within the family unit, and some of the challenges that can arise within neurodiverse households, particularly looking at sibling relationships and parenting approaches as areas of importance. Our goal for you, as parents of autistic girls and gender diverse young people, is to feel seen, supported and empowered to make your home a neuro-affirming environment where your children know they are safe and accepted.

UNDERSTANDING BEHAVIOUR

Behaviour is one of the most misunderstood and challenging aspects of raising autistic young people. Because your home can be your child's safe place, you may be experiencing repeated, intense behaviours from your children, often not witnessed by others.

When your ladybug is exhibiting challenging behaviours (these may either be externalised fight or flight reactions, or internalised freeze or fawn reactions, or a combination of both), it is understandable that their heightened distressed state leads you to increasingly become stressed yourself. You may also find that any attempts you make to calm you or your ladybug down, do not work, or in fact escalate the situation. At this point, you might be getting desperate to resolve the situation, and even resort to offering bribes, making threats or giving punishments to gain back some control. This, however, is ineffective. Let us explain why.

> *Their frontal lobe is offline. So, your attempts to 'rein in the behaviour' by using conventional techniques, such as time-outs, reward charts, etc., will not work in the heat of the moment.*

Our starting point for understanding behaviour is to not actually focus on the behaviour itself but see it as a signal that something else is going on. When an autistic child's brain is in a heightened distress state and complex behaviours are occurring, it is important to understand that their brain is no longer in complete control of their behavioural or emotional responses. For them in that moment, the disruption, running, throwing, screaming or whatever else they are doing, all makes sense because they are reacting to a perceived threat. No amount of logic is going to calm them down in that moment, because they have lost the ability to self-regulate and rationalise – their frontal lobe is offline. So, your attempts to 'rein in the behaviour' by using conventional techniques, such as time-outs, reward charts, etc., will not work in the heat of the moment. Instead of looking at complex and challenging behaviour as problematic and something that needs to be fixed, we need to instead be asking the question 'what is that behaviour telling us about the child?' (see Dr Mona Delahooke). What is happening within your child's environment that they are finding stressful? Or what are their unmet needs?

It is important to remember that distressed behaviour, including meltdowns and shutdowns are means of communication, and that during a meltdown, your ladybug is not trying to give you a hard time – they are going through a hard time. You are their safe space where they can let their guard down and express their true feelings in the moment. And we get it – it can be really hard. Being on the frontline and the safe person isn't easy, especially when trying to regulate your own reactions. Though you may not be able to stop a meltdown once it has started, there are strategies that can be implemented within the home which will help you feel more confident and enable your child to feel safer and less overwhelmed.

We love the following insight from autistic advocate Allison Davies:

> 'The biggest game-changer for me personally was when I started to think of having a meltdown as being part of a cycle. The meltdown itself wasn't what I needed to focus on, or the thing that I needed to manage or fix. The meltdown was simply the result of not meeting my own needs, or the needs of my children. I started shifting my focus away from the meltdowns themselves, and started focusing on what could be done to better support me, and my family, and I learned that meltdowns are not the problem. Meltdowns are simply the by-product of a whole realm of overwhelm that is going on.'

AUTISTIC-APPROVED STRATEGIES TO SUPPORT COMPLEX BEHAVIOUR

At Yellow Ladybugs, our biggest 'call for help' is mostly centred around strategies that help reduce complex and distressing behaviours. And for good reason. We love our children, and we don't want to see them stressed, overwhelmed and in pain. As a parent, it can also be so overwhelming to find and secure the right help. We often exhaust ourselves, constantly searching for answers, questioning ourselves and the decisions we make, and sometimes end up more confused than when we begin. Remind yourself that best practice, therapies and preferred language is constantly evolving. We live in a culture where we often fear making the wrong choice and being judged for that. It's important to remember that we are doing all we can with the information we have. Focusing on autistic-approved strategies and practices is always the best place to start.

One autistic parent shared with us that it is not easy to get right, and their experience with the cycle of over-thinking and second-guessing:

> 'My mind doesn't rest. It's constantly looking, searching, and trying to find the right support for my teen. It's trying to change a world that sometimes just doesn't get it – get them. It's constantly second-guessing decisions I've made and wondering

if I've done enough – or too much. It's stressed about the past, present, and future all at once. It's all of this and more. And worse, it's probably only 5 per cent of what they are experiencing. If I'm finding it this hard, I can't imagine what they are going through.'

The good (and maybe bad?) news is that you play a much bigger role than you might think. With the right tools, you will feel more confident to support your ladybug, but you also need to work on you. Co-regulation is going to be critical when using all the strategies we have listed below. And for those who want a quick cheat sheet on what co-regulation means – think of it like this: 'your aim is to pull your ladybug into your calm, not join their chaos'.

Acknowledging what your ladybug is feeling and validating what they are going through is going to be key. Remember the mantra: If they could they would. It helps remind you in the heat of the moment.

So, what do you need to do? You need to build your own capacity to self-regulate and avoid escalating things, before you expect your ladybug to try and do something that you are not modelling yourself. This might open a Pandora's box of stress, concerns and issues for you, as we know many of us also have our own unmet needs and challenges. But this is your chance to let you know you are worth it. And it will not only help you, but your family. Knowing you are not alone can help, as this autistic parent shared with us:

'I'm beginning to understand how much inner work I need to do on me, and it's confronting. I've always been an empath, but it's become so much more intense since becoming a mum. When they feel happy, I feel ecstatic, when they feel sad, I feel broken. I know it's not their burden to bear, and I need to work this out. But I can sense my past, all the unhealed parts of me, chasing and finally catching up with me. I see my history in the reflection of their eyes. I don't want history to repeat itself, so maybe I am putting too much pressure on myself to fix things for her, so I don't need to face my own memories. What I know for sure, is that it's scary, painful and it consumes me. But I know it will be worth it.'

Below are some popular strategies that we use to help build up that trust, connection and safety with our children within our home environments. They will also give you some techniques that you can practise when you are not in the heat of the situation, so you can better self-regulate and move closer to co-regulation.

UNCONDITIONAL POSITIVE REGARD

Unconditional positive regard is the assumption that your ladybug is doing the best that they can with what they have available. If they are struggling or acting out, even if their actions seem deliberate, you can assume that they are coping to the best of their ability, acknowledging what they are feeling in the moment, and validating what they are going through. A mantra we often use is, *if they could they would*. Positive regard can be really difficult to maintain, especially when continuous and repetitive behaviours of concern recur without change. But whenever you notice yourself slipping into judgement or criticism, remember to separate your child from the action and keep focusing on acceptance.

When your child feels like you are listening to them and their feelings are being validated, you develop deeper trust and connection, which helps them to feel safe and can speed up de-escalation. You are then able to work out with your ladybug why these challenging behaviours are occurring and develop a plan to assist them in the future. For more on this, see Dr Ross Greene's Collaborative and Proactive Solutions (CPS) model.

PACE

PACE (DPP network, Dr Alberto Veloso) stands for playfulness, acceptance, curiosity and empathy, and for many parents in our community has become the go-to strategy for knowing how to react in stressful situations at home. It has been a game changer in so many of our families because it provides the structure and guidance to respond in a safer way without escalating things. So what does PACE mean?

Playfulness

Stressed brains respond to calm, playful faces and tones of voice. For those ladybugs who are in tune and hyper aware of their surroundings, it is especially important to be aware of your tone or expressions – even neutral tones can seem threatening. When a child is beginning to experience stress, one way to counter this is to introduce playfulness into the situation. This can be something as simple as sitting and engaging in a conversation about what they are doing, or cracking a joke. Implementing playfulness can defuse arousal, reduce conflict and increase connectiveness, all of which aid in reducing escalation.

Acceptance

Acceptance is openly communicating with your ladybug that you accept their feelings, thoughts, urges and perceptions completely, and trusting that what they are feeling is their truth in that moment. When young people know that they are being heard, they will be more likely to let down their defences and allow for connection to occur. Acceptance can also mean that you radically accept whatever is in front of you and focus on supporting your ladybug through the situation, regardless of how it might trigger you. For example, your ladybug throws their pencils all over the floor, just after you cleaned up. Acceptance would look beyond your own frustration (we use a mantra: 'it is what it is') and focus on the next step: why.

The biggest game changer is when you embrace the concept of 'connection over correction' and lead with empathy and curiosity.

Curiosity

Curiosity is being curious about where the behaviour has come from by truly trying to understand your child's perspective. This is achieved by asking them open-ended questions – or contemplating these questions yourself. By allowing children to speak openly, you let the child know that they are being heard. Curiosity can also promote their own self-reflection on their feelings and behaviour. This self-reflection can help with de-escalation. Following on from the above example, we might find out that they lost a game they were really invested in, and their friend has teased them about it. So, onto the next step ...

Empathy

This is where you can genuinely attempt to understand your child's position. By demonstrating that you understand how difficult an experience might be for them, you are comforting them and letting them know they do not have to deal with their distress alone. In the example earlier, we can say 'It's hard when things don't go our way' or 'I am here to be with you' or 'That really hurt, didn't it?' By focusing on connection (over or before) correction, we are reducing the risk for further escalation and building safer home environments.

TWO-HANDED APPROACH TO SETTING BOUNDARIES

Establishing the 'connection over correction' philosophy in your home, does not mean children can just do whatever they want. Rules and limits should be in place, so your ladybug is aware of the boundaries. Side note: Rules and consequences should be fair, logical and consistent to help your ladybug feel safe and have predictability. Your goal in establishing these boundaries, rules and consequences is to always balance them alongside building and maintaining a safe and supportive connection.

The two-handed approach works like a balance scale, where you want both sides to be equal. With one hand, you provide your boundaries and limitations, and with the other, connectiveness and support. For example, you might have set the limit of the iPad to finish at bedtime. Instead of taking the iPad and saying, 'Too bad, you knew the rules', you might sit with them, connect with what they are playing with, ask them some questions, and then take the iPad away. If (and probably when) they get upset, it's best to connect and say, 'I know, it's really hard stopping doing what we like. I can sit here with you until you feel better.' This is a simple example, but you can see how you are not only setting the limit, but using your relationship and connection in a way that balances it out. The more limits and boundaries that are in place, the more you need to increase your connectiveness.

When you have a child that needs more limits within the home or school setting, you also need to ramp up the playfulness to match those demands. When those two levels are balanced, distress begins to decrease.

It is
what
it is.

RADICAL ACCEPTANCE

Radical acceptance means choosing to parent in the way that works best for your family, rather than following societal expectations and pressures. It is about recognising individual struggles and embracing individual needs within the family by saying 'mine and my children's mental health are more important than what society wants, so I am going to raise my children the way that works best for them, so that their mental health is protected'. By acknowledging individual struggles within the home environment and changing the things that are causing undue harm and distress, you are ultimately helping to create a safe space for your child.

One neurodivergent parent shared their experience with radical acceptance:

> 'It has taken some people within our support network a long time to truly understand what we mean when we talk about radical acceptance. Sometimes we want to participate but we need to do what is best for our family. Our children manage their own bedrooms and are allowed to do messy sensory activities in the safety of their bedrooms. Many people completely freak out when they see the state of their rooms! However, for our children this has such a huge positive impact on them feeling safe and calm and in control of their own space.'

CREATING A SAFE, AUTISTIC-AFFIRMING HOME ENVIRONMENT

One of the best things you can do for your autistic young person is to give them a safe place where they know they are unconditionally loved and are accepted for being exactly who they are meant to be. But what does an autistic-affirming home environment look like, and how can you create a space that is supportive and inclusive of their needs?

Below are some suggestions and strategies that you can implement within your home to help you support your ladybug.

ACCEPTING AUTISM

The process of formally getting your child identified as autistic can be incredibly difficult and full of emotions. And as we know, for girls and gender diverse young people, this process can be even harder. For some parents, a diagnosis can be a huge relief. For others, it can cause fear and uncertainty for the future.

Know that your ladybug is not broken and in need of being fixed. They are neurodivergent, and as the absolutely wonderful autistic advocate and Yellow Ladybugs ambassador, Chloe Hayden, says, they are exactly who they are meant to be. They need to know that you love and accept them for who they are, and that means accepting that they are neurodivergent. Learn about autism from actually autistic voices, and celebrate their differences. After all, the world would be pretty boring if we were all the same.

DO NOT HIDE THEIR IDENTITY

On that note, tell your autistic children that they are autistic. Many autistic children know that they are different and hiding their identity can perpetuate their loneliness and isolation; impacting their mental health. Telling them that they are autistic does not put a 'label' on them. It helps give them a better understanding of their neurology and opens the door to learning about themselves and connecting with their neurokin as well.

You can start by explaining to your ladybug that all brains are different, and that each brain has strengths and challenges. Reducing the stigma of neurodivergence at home is the first step to your child growing and accepting who they are. In Chapter 6, Embracing an autistic identity and culture, you'll find much more on this subject, but in the meantime, please listen to autistic mother, and psychologist Sandhya Menon, talking about a more nuanced approach to this topic:

> *'The research is clear – tell your child they're autistic. When children know their identity and can make sense of their experiences, this serves as a protective factor for further mental health struggles down the track. Yet, this journey can be ... hard. We need to unpack our own internalised ableism about what being*

autistic means and set a new pathway forward for the next generation to embrace autistic identity. Furthermore, for inter-dependent cultures who pride themselves on belonging and relying to community, the idea of self-referencing can be a jolt. These cultures might describe autistic behaviour as selfish, and therefore finding out we're autistic, whilst true, may feel shameful or guilt inducing. Tension exists between their cultural identity and their autistic identity. These individuals face greater challenges in uncovering their autistic identity as they straddle the two worlds and navigate reaching a pathway and identity that feels right for them. This may not be what the dominant autistic culture provides, but it is perhaps on the onus of the dominant autistic culture to take into account. In our quest for inclusion for neurominorities, it is absolutely essential for us to bring our cultural minorities along with us and make space for them in embracing autistic culture.'

'Children deserve to know what their neurotype is, and find their way to community when they're ready. It's important to know their experience has a name, and that they're not alone in their journey.'
– Sandhya Menon

ENCOURAGING PASSIONS AND STRENGTHS

Like so many of their neurokin, autistic girls and gender diverse young people have intense interests and passions. One of the main strengths of autism is the ability to hyperfocus, and many autistic people are known to develop strong special interests. Embrace your ladybug's passions, or better yet, join in with them! By encouraging and supporting these passions, you show your child that what they care about matters.

UNDERSTANDING DIFFERENCES IN AUTISTIC COMMUNICATION

Communication styles for many autistic people can look different to neurotypicals. Here are some differences and neuro-affirming strategies that can help support autistic children within the home environment.

STIMMING

As we mentioned in the first chapter of this book, stimming is a form of autistic body language. One of the ways many autistic children, and indeed adults, too, communicate is through their stimming. Stimming – the repetition of physical movements, sounds, or the movement of an object – provides autistics with a means of emotional regulation, sensory stimulation, or is done as a means of expression. Many autistics will stim as a means of communication, with stims showing excitement, anxiousness, fear, etc.

Stimming is the body's way to help regulate emotions. Therefore, it is important to not stop your autistic young person from stimming, providing that the stim is not hurting themself or others. If your child is stimming, their body is trying to self-regulate.

EYE CONTACT

For many neurotypicals, maintaining eye contact during a conversation is a sign that a person is engaged and listening, and not maintaining eye contact during a conversation is often seen as rude.

For many autistic people, eye contact can, at best, be uncomfortable, and for some, can cause physical pain and overload. Your ladybug may find that they are able to take information in better when they are not forced to look into your eyes.

Do not force or try to teach eye contact. Just because they are not looking at you, does not mean they are not hearing you. Their lack of eye contact may in fact mean the opposite: they are trying to focus on what you are saying.

BE DIRECT

Many of our ladybugs can struggle with non-verbal forms of communication. Deciphering body language, reading facial expressions, picking up on sarcasm, and reading non-verbal social cues can all be very difficult.

To make the home environment less confusing, be direct when you talk with your ladybug. If you want them to clean their room, tell them explicitly that they need to clean their room. Better still, give them pointers on exactly what you would like cleaned. The clearer and more direct you can be, the more your autistic young person will be able to follow what you say.

LITERAL THINKING

It is important to remember that many autistic people are very literal. We will tell you how it is (often with very little sugar-coating), and we will likewise expect that what you are saying is what you mean. If you are not being completely literal, your ladybug may not understand your intentions.

PROCESSING TIME

Your ladybug may need extra processing time, even if they are extremely verbal or chatty, or talk very fast themselves. Therefore, if you ask a question or request something, do not expect an immediate answer or action, as they may need time to process. Bear in mind that this might mean an extra minute or two, or it could mean days. Sometimes it can help to ask if they might like you to rephrase the question rather than simply repeating what you have asked – sometimes if we hit a 'road block' this can help.

MINIMISING SENSORY OVERWHELM WITHIN THE HOME

One of the biggest challenges faced by autistic people is the sensory overload that can come from living in a world not designed for us. Sensory overload occurs when your body's senses become overstimulated. Instead of adapting to the stimuli, many autistic people can become overwhelmed. If the sensory exposure continues, the body will turn to fight or flight mode, often resulting in a meltdown or shutdown.

> *We might seem calm on the surface, but like a duck on the water, we are paddling furiously underneath just to stay afloat.*

Sensory overload is one of the main reasons many autistic young people, at the end of a school day, will meltdown or shutdown once they are home. This is especially the case for ladybugs who have a more internalised presentation and may have been masking or 'holding in' their sensory discomfort throughout the school day.

There are a number of ways you can help reduce sensory overwhelm for your ladybug within the home:

DECOMPRESSION TIME

Following a stressful day or event (even if it is something that they enjoy), allow your child time to decompress. Recognise that there is a recharge that needs to happen following events like school, social engagements and outings. During this time, it is best to reduce the demands placed on your young person, and allow them to engage in an activity that they enjoy and find relaxing. This helps to reduce sensory overwhelm that can lead to melt-downs and shutdowns.

One autistic adult in our community described their experience of social overwhelm:

> 'A social hangover feels a bit like having too much to drink. You are fatigued afterwards, you may feel weak, have sensitivity to light and sounds, a headache and need to sleep it off. But it can also leave your soul feeling heavy for days, as you've absorbed everyone's energy like a sponge. You can get dizzy from over-thinking every chat you had.'

ESTABLISHING ROUTINES

Many ladybugs struggle with change and thrive from the predict-ability of routines. Establishing routines can help your child feel safe and secure within their home environment and create deeper trust between you both.

Some routines can be established simply through repetition. Other children may benefit from visual prompts that they can use as a guide. Using charts that children can check off tasks, utilising alarms and adding visual countdown timers are just some examples of how you can develop a routine within the home. These things can also support a child's executive function. Some autistic young people, especially those who experience significant anxiety, may benefit from developing the routine themselves. Often it takes trial and error to find an approach that is best suited to the individual child's specific needs.

Establishing routines can help create order in both your child's life and yours. They can be used to assist your child with daily tasks like getting ready for school or bed, self-care, and general day-to-day happenings. When your child knows what to expect, they are more likely to feel secure and have a sense of stability, which can aid in their overall self-regulation.

HANDLING CHANGE

Change can be hard for many ladybugs. Some autistic young people become so immersed in what they are doing that stopping is both emotionally and physically difficult. Others find comfort and safety in what they are doing, or the way things are, and the prospect of change can induce fear and anxiety.

Though your ladybug may always struggle with the idea of change, there are strategies you can implement which may help make transitions easier for them.

- Prepare them for what is to come by explaining to them what is going to happen and when. By breaking down for them how things are going to work, you can ease feelings of suddenness, fear and anxiety that can come with change.

- Use visual aids. This could include schedules or calendars that are accessible around the house that detail what is going to happen with timers to help with transitions (although we note that for some autistic young people, timers may cause anxiety, and a more indirect countdown method may be preferable).

- Give them a safe space where they can decompress if they are feeling anxious or frustrated with a change.

- Utilise social stories, developed by Carol Gray, where applicable. There are apps and websites that will help you to create social stories to assist your child, and a simple Google search will often bring up past social stories that others have used around a particular subject. Please note that social stories work best when they are factual and reassuring, and they should never place behavioural expectations on children.

- Accept that your child may struggle with transitions and changes. Assure them that their feelings are valid and you are there to support them.

ADDITIONAL TOOLS AND STRATEGIES

There are additional strategies that can help a child deal with some of the sensory overwhelm within the home.

- Self-care: This is one of the most challenging aspects of home life for autistic children and adults. Many parents have expressed frustration that their ladybug is not brushing their teeth or hair, showering, getting enough sleep and taking care of the logistics of menstrual cycles. On the surface, these seem like simple tasks, but the reality is they require significant executive functioning and can cause sensory overwhelm. Get to know what works for your ladybug. Visual aids and sensory-friendly items (such as period underwear, soft brushes, nice-flavoured toothpaste) can help, but in some cases the most important strategy of all is being curious, connected and using empathy to understand why they may find these particular areas difficult. Throw in a dash of radical acceptance – 'it is what it is' – and you will be on the right track.

- Sensory-friendly clothing: Tags, buttons, stitching, fabric and fit can all be sensory nightmares for autistic children and adults. Sourcing sensory-friendly clothing, and allowing your ladybug to wear the clothes that they feel comfortable in, can help reduce sensory overload. This may mean purchasing the same item in multiples.

- Calming spaces can be instrumental in helping to reduce overwhelm. This could be a corner in their bedroom where they have a tent, a beanbag, soft cushions, stimming toys and other quiet activities that can help them to self-regulate. It doesn't need to be big or fancy. It just needs to be a space where they feel safe.

- Noise-cancelling headphones or ear defenders can be a simple and effective measure to help reduce sensory stimulation. There are various designs available, and you may need to try several until you discover what your ladybug finds most comfortable.

- Simple adjustments like dimming lights, turning off appliances, reducing noise volume, and removing other distractions can be very helpful in managing sensory overload.

The above are some autistic-supported suggestions of things you can put in place to help create a space within your home where your ladybug feels safe, and where their sensory and emotional needs are met. We at Yellow Ladybugs encourage you to continue to learn and discover what works best for your family members.

FAMILY DYNAMICS

SUPPORTING YOURSELF

It can at times be very difficult to find a balance between your own needs and the needs of your child. This is regardless of whether you are neurotypical or autistic or otherwise neurodivergent yourself. Competing sensory needs between you and your children can sometimes lead to you as a parent feeling overloaded or overwhelmed.

You are not perfect. No one is. Remember that, because there will be days you lose your cool. You might say the words that shouldn't be said. It is often when we are in our own triggered, impulsive and heightened state that we get to these points. And that makes sense. We are juggling our own requirements and many of us need to become more aware of our internal state and triggers. Parenting sure does bring all of that to the forefront. Please know that having lapses in judgement still means that you are a good parent, and that you love your child. You can make mistakes and still be a loving, caring and wonderful parent. Both things can be true. What is important is how you then focus on repairing and nurturing your relationship with your ladybug so you both feel safe.

One autistic mother shared:

'I'm not going to lie, I am finding it hard to balance my own needs, and much-needed downtime, with the demands of family life. I don't feel seen or even understood. I am constantly trying to stay calm and avoid my own meltdowns. I'm still trying to figure out my own triggers, and don't have the time or energy to explore, let alone receive the support I desperately need. I'm running on an empty tank, but I know it's time to begin filling it.'

You are
so loved.

AN IMPORTANT NOTE ON THE TEEN YEARS

No discussion about your own wellbeing is complete without looking at strategies to survive parenting the teen years. Without sounding like 'woe is me', martyr-type parents, it must be said that between the ages of 13 and 15, things can especially be tricky for our ladybugs and so too our role as a parent and our relationship with them. It is healthy for children to begin seeking more independence from you. You might find the shift in your relationship difficult to navigate, especially where you've previously been their fierce advocate and their safe person – to now potentially being their main trigger or stressor. It might feel like you are being cast aside and rejected. This can hurt, even more for those of us with highly sensitive souls or rejection sensitivity. You may feel depleted (especially if you are an empath), continually witnessing wave after wave of emotions from your ladybug, which can stir up your own past traumas and experiences. Understandably, this can really bring up a range of emotions, especially for those of us with anxiety or other conditions, and therefore requires proactive and specific support.

It is okay to acknowledge that you also need time to support your own mental health. In fact, this is essential. Seek out support when needed, from family and friends, your general practitioner (GP), allied health professionals or even closed online support groups. Take time for yourself, do something that you enjoy, and utilise any external resources that can help make your life easier. When you are feeling safe, this will trickle down to your family and help with their regulation as well. And don't be afraid to do what works for your family to protect yours and your children's mental wellbeing.

One neurodivergent carer shared their thoughts with us:

'It's a pain I've not felt in years. Decades even. It took me right back to high school. To the days when I was scared, alone and the target of all their hate. The mean girls, who wanted nothing to do with me, and seemed to show no remorse for the impact they were making. I know my child is not them. I know she loves me deep down. But she's been so hard on me. I know most mother – teen relationships can get tricky, but this feels like another level. I don't know what I can do to make things better. I know all the theory and logic: she is going through a tough time, and I am her safe place. But it hurts. And I wonder If I am ever going to be enough for her. I know that's my anxiety talking, so I will lick my wounds and take comfort in knowing nothing she can ever do will ever make me love her any less. And that keeps me going.'

MANAGING DIFFERENT PARENTING OR CARER STYLES

Different parenting styles can further complicate how you support your ladybug, making it much more difficult to create harmony in the home. You might not even be aware of your parenting style, and if and how it may differ from your partner and/or family. If this is the case, we suggest you do further research on this topic and even include a look at your values. If your styles align, and it is working for you and your ladybug: great! If you are finding this area particularly confronting and frustrating, you are not alone. Many of our families adopt the tuned-in, gentle and connected parenting style that we showcase throughout this book. We hear so many parents express concern that their partner or extended family do not mirror this approach and take a more authoritative stance when trying to support their ladybug. This is a topic that comes up frequently within the Yellow Ladybugs community – what do you do when one parent is using discipline and authority to try and alter 'behaviour', making the home feel unsafe for their autistic child?

Whist each situation is different, and we are not here to solve this particular issue for you, we think it is important to begin with a more balanced and nuanced approach. Firstly, it is important not to panic. Even if you are the only one adopting a connected and safe approach, there will be huge benefits for your ladybug. Your understanding, connection and secure and safe attachment style will build a strong foundation for them. Secondly, it may be helpful to use the very same strategies that you have learnt to use with your ladybug, to support your partner or family. Be curious: why is your partner or family holding onto this approach or belief? There might be many factors that contribute to their current beliefs and parenting style. This could include family history or trauma, cultural and society expectations, their values, their own attachment insecurities or wounds, an internalised sense of shame, rejection sensitivity to alternative ideas and potential demand avoidance themselves. This might be a good time to remind yourself that autism is hereditary, and it might explain why so many of us have trouble with change, emotion regulation and impulsivity. This is not an excuse, however, for behaviour that becomes verbally or physically abusive. Safety needs to be prioritised and if this is the case, please seek out professional help in your local area.

WORKING TOGETHER

Once you have a better understanding of everyone's perspective, it is now the time to work out how you might collaborate, and problem solve regarding how (and if) you can get on the same page. This needs to be done in a respectful and non-judgemental way so everyone feels safe before any guidance or advice is given. It is important not to compare where you are at with your journey of understanding with your partner or family. Be patient and appreciate it may take time.

Here are some further tips and strategies to help you get on the same page with your partner and/or family:

- Communication, communication, communication: as clichéd as this sounds, this really is going to be the most important part of this process. Think outside the square – find a place, time and method that works for you both. Is it via text message? On a drive alone? If you need help from a professional, such as a family therapist, now is the time to invest your time and energy into it.

- Be united: try to agree how you might approach situations before they happen. It's easier said than done, but it's a good reminder.

- Attend your child's therapist sessions together: encourage your partner to ask as many questions as they want.

- Invite them to join you in listening to your favourite neuro-affirming podcasts or share any relevant books you find useful.

- Provide them with the 'why': for example, show them the benefit using a gentle, connected, and nurturing parenting style can make. Be careful not to 'I told you so' it to death, as this will just breed defensiveness.

- Reflect on situations together when things are calm.

- Use a 'tag' system: pass control over to your partner and vice versa, when you notice each other escalating

Hopefully the guidance above has helped you. However, if you begin to realise that things are still not working, it is important to remember that you are ultimately not responsible for the relationship between your child and your partner.

SUPPORTING SIBLING RELATIONSHIPS

The dynamics of sibling relationships can be complicated in all families, but when one or more of your children are autistic, it can add new challenges that you never expected. Sibling relationships will change over time, and can be influenced by a variety of factors, including their current age, personality, family circumstances, communication needs, and external factors, such as friends, stressors, activities – the list can go on.

In our experience, we have found that one of the greatest factors that can complicate sibling relationships is their competing needs (and this happens whether the siblings are either also autistic or not). An example may be that your ladybug might have misophonia (the extreme reaction to particular day-to-day sounds) while their sibling may enjoy verbally stimming. Conflict. Your ladybug could be a sensory seeker, preferring loud music, bright lights and seeking multiple sensory stimuli. Whilst their sibling requires quiet, calm, and a peaceful environment. Conflict. And to keep you all on your toes, it can change weekly, daily or even hourly. This can put a strain on their relationship, opening many gateways to distress and tension. For parents, managing these conflicting needs can be extremely difficult, especially if they clash with your own sensory needs as well. It is important to reinforce with your children that everyone has different needs, preferences and communication styles, and each are valid. Empowering your children to speak up with what they need, in a respectful and safe way, also helps. In our experience, it is useful to provide safe spaces or multiple zones within the home, where each person can retreat and attend to their individual sensory needs. It would be impossible for us to list every potential challenge or conflict when it comes to sibling relationships. However, we have shared some of the more common challenges that we have heard and experienced at Yellow Ladybugs, when it comes to sibling dynamics of our autistic girls and gender diverse children.

Distressed behaviour is often overwhelming to observe and can impact the mental health of family and support networks.

THE IMPACT OF OBSERVING
DISTRESSED BEHAVIOUR

While much of our focus in this book has been on internalised autism, some ladybugs also experience extreme externalised behaviour, and the reality is that witnessing others in the home externalising their emotions can be distressing. For example, your ladybug may repeatedly witness their sibling go through extreme and violent meltdowns. This situation may cause a range of emotions for your ladybug, including fear, anxiety and even animosity. Watching a meltdown can be scary, and there may be sensory overwhelm associated with listening and seeing a meltdown. For our ladybugs who are empaths or problem solvers, their distress can be because it is upsetting, confusing or frustrating, or because they are constantly searching for a solution. Witnessing a meltdown can affect their mental health, as they have such a strong compassion towards their sibling – it hurts. They might even feel invisible, and begin to get angry, sensing their own silent shutdowns tend to go unnoticed.

As a parent, it is a delicate and difficult balancing act, trying to meet all needs in the family, and sometimes you are naturally drawn to the more 'obvious' need. Your ladybug may perceive your actions as unfair, especially if they have a passion for equality and justice. So, it is important to remember that even if one of your children internalises their emotions, their feelings are still just as important as their sibling/s whose emotions may be more outward. Just because your ladybug might be quiet, does not mean they are not struggling. It is therefore important to check in on them and give them some individual time and support as well.

CHANGING DYNAMICS

As your children get older and especially as they enter their teen years, the dynamics between siblings can rapidly shift. Your ladybug might be going through (or witnessing their sibling go through) lots of physical, emotional and psychological changes. The changes might involve puberty, a greater reliance on outside friendship groups, more mature interests, going out and wearing new clothes. These changes can feel threating or unsafe to your ladybug and might put a strain on their sibling relationships. Although this process cannot be stopped (nor should it), it can help to explain or discuss what is going on. Helping siblings to connect occasionally through new shared interests and experiences can help foster acceptance of the change.

As a neurodivergent family, it was hard for all of us, trying to walk on eggshells, hoping to avoid another conflict.

One neurodivergent parent in our community summed up these changing dynamics well:

'I noticed my daughter became quite moody before her periods set in, and it really intensified one they established. This was really hard for her to go through but did impact the entire family. It was hard for all of us, trying to walk on eggshells, hoping to

avoid another conflict. We wanted the best for her, but this was
such a change to what we were all used to. It was helpful to track
her periods with her, so we could prepare her and encourage her
siblings to be more gentle and also remind ourselves not to take
it personally.'

NEGATIVE SIBLING MIMICRY

Many ladybugs are empaths and keen observers. Seeing your sibling go through mental health issues can be very distressing, and the impact this may have on them cannot be minimised. We have heard from our community that some ladybugs have witnessed their siblings go through situations such as self-harm, eating disorders and suicidal ideation, and it may have possibly led to them mimicking similar concerning behaviours. Often these issues are very difficult to navigate and tease out. Don't be afraid to seek outside professional help.

EXTENDED FAMILY
AND FAMILY FRIENDS

There can be no greater comfort than having a close group of family and friends who understand, appreciate and support you and your family. But what do we do when this isn't the case? Our community members have often shared their disappointment and frustration with their family and friends, who not only judge their parenting, but also question their ladybug's autism. How do we strengthen our network of friends and family, without adding further stress into our lives? Whilst it is not our job to teach our family and friends how to be supportive and inclusive, it is helpful to remember that not everyone will be at your level of understanding. Be patient and meet them where they are at. Although, this is also a good time to remind yourself that some relationships may simply be too damaging to subject your children to and it really is your choice.

One member shared with us:

> 'We have had to make decisions that if certain family cannot respect the language choices my ladybug has made around their pronouns, then it may be time to take some space from that particular situation or relationship. Even though I come from a strong ethnic family, where family means everything, I need to model that boundary for them. It might not be forever, and they may be doing their best, but I trust my decision, because I know I have given enough of an opportunity for them to change and do better.'

One of the best things you can do to support your child, is to practise putting you and your ladybug's needs first. This might be uncomfortable at the start, especially for those of us who people please to avoid the extended family drama and conflict.

Having healthy
boundaries
is a form of
self-love
and
self-respect.

It is going to be important for you to show your children how to advocate for themselves. You can model this by letting your family know what your needs and boundaries are. It is okay to say no to friends and family events that you know will make your ladybug uncomfortable. It is okay to end a discussion where you are feeling judged. It is okay to be selective with who and how you spend your time as a family.

Here are some examples, showing how you can be firm and fair when expressing your boundaries:

- 'I'm not comfortable talking about that'.
- 'That's not going to work for us. We need Sunday for rest days.'
- 'We can attend for a short time, but my ladybug will be using the back room for downtime on their device.'
- 'We don't make our ladybug to do hugs and kisses.'

It is also important to note that each family is different and unique, and when exploring ways to navigate these relationships, you will need to consider your own culture, needs and values.

One Yellow Ladybug parent shared:

'If one more therapist asks me why we choose not to sit down as a family my eyes might roll out of my head. We are a family that consists of multiple autistic children and parents and siblings of other neurodivergent identities including two of us that have misophonia. Whenever I am probed from therapists about "family dinners" my mind turns to the orchestra on the Titanic, diligently playing the final song as the Titanic sinks, fulfilling their obligations rather than saving themselves! As our family grew, it became very clear that each of us had our own sensory triggers – even us parents, and that a group dinnertime was often distressing for our children and simply not a priority! Noises around dinnertime can be extremely triggering and for others the smells and forced conversation does not result in positive family bonding time. Instead for us, acknowledging what we all need to function is a way of building trust and acceptance within our family unit. I consider this a way of saving ourselves! We do on occasions enjoy dinner outside in the backyard as a family – moving around, taking breaks as needed with no set expectations. For neurodivergent families often spending time in the same space but not directly engaging is a great way of supporting each other. In a nutshell, don't go down with the ship. Do what works to keep your family afloat.'

UNSOLICITED ADVICE

You will almost certainly encounter unsolicited advice from family, friends, colleagues and probably even the bus driver. This is unfortunately quite common and depending on where you are on your journey it can be upsetting for your ladybug and for yourself.

A good example is when people might preach about limiting screen time. Maybe you've managed to get your entire family to a group dinner, you are pleased, your kids are settled and one child needs some screen time to help them self-regulate. You are proud that they have identified that themselves and you give over the iPad since it is a great tool for your child when they are in a loud overwhelming environment. You are really thrilled that you are all together and out for dinner with friends. Then someone makes a comment about kids not having conversations at the table anymore, they suggest too much screen time is why kids can't sit still and some tough love and green juice would get you back on track. Of course, this is none of their business and you have not asked them for advice. A strong response can be: 'if it doesn't bother me then it should not bother you'. Then you should make it clear to your ladybug that you are proud that they are with you and you are happy they have the tools to keep themselves regulated!

Unsolicited advice will come in many forms and over time you will find what works for you, but always remember you are in charge of advocating for your ladybug. You know your child and what they need.

One member of our community shared:

> 'Once, at the movies, our ladybug needed to take their shoes off as they were hurting. It was no issue at all for me or for them. They ran around on the carpet and were very happy. A woman approached me who was visibly upset that my child had no shoes on. She kept talking at me about looking after my child. We were on carpet and there was literally no risk at all to my child. I was genuinely confused as to why so much fuss. I turned to my ladybug and said, "who made her the shoe police?" and off we went to get our movie snacks.'

OUTSIDE HELP

The reality is, for many of us, we just might not have a close circle of friends or family we can rely on to get through the day to day. Many within our community are solo parents or carers, which is even more reason to look beyond and explore opportunities for help outside the family. Suffice to say, many lean on their ladybugs' allied health team, including speech pathologists, occupational therapists, psychologists, family therapists, mental health case managers, as well as psychiatrists, GPs and a host of other health professionals, for the same comfort, understanding and connection we all crave. There are also options, if you are adequately funded with support for peer workers, who will not only give your ladybug a sense of connection, but help you feel less isolated. You might also think about connecting with school staff or other parents within your school community who make you and your ladybug feel safe (and yes, we do understand that sometimes it can be even more isolating when other parents don't understand your reality, even if they mean well). But if you can find safe, empathetic people in this setting, then they can be a great source of support. Other ideas include expanding your reach safely online, through local parenting groups or joining local face-to-face parenting groups.

Whoever you choose, consider all the same tips and strategies above around boundaries, and prioritise those people who are affirming to your family values and understand autistic culture – which you can learn more about in our final chapter.

CONCLUSION

In a world not designed for autistic individuals, home is the place where autistic girls and gender diverse young people are likely to feel the most comfortable, secure, and able to be true to their authentic self. Although family dynamics and being a neurodiverse or neurodivergent household can come with unique challenges, you can encourage this feeling of safety by learning to understand autistic communication, utilising autistic-approved strategies for building connections with your young people and helping to minimise sensory overload while embracing who they are as autistic individuals. When your children know they can be who they truly are at home, and know that they are accepted, that is when you will see what they are capable of and their confidence as neurodivergent young people will grow.

MINI INTERVIEW:
CHERIE CLONAN,
CEO, THE DIGITAL PICNIC

Growing up, what do you wish your parent/s had understood about you?

I consider myself to be a really lucky little autiste, who was raised by an #ActuallyAutistic, fierce male feminist single father.

My childhood was neuro-affirmative perfection: I was seen for the person that I am. I was celebrated. He focused on all of my autistic strengths and didn't pathologise my 'deficits', and he set up our home to be a sensory wonderland (dim lighting, really quiet, calm, peaceful, and all of the things I needed to be happy: think plush toys and dolls).

He advocated for me. Gently, and then fiercely (when I got to high school, and was subjected to horrific bullying).

I'd wish my incredible autistic dad on *every* autistic child.

What do you wish your teachers had understood about you?

I was your 'formally assessed, high IQ' kinda autie girl at school … but I was forgotten.

My teachers were barely aware that I existed. I was quiet, daydreamy, I got the marks, I passed the assignments, and I presented no challenges … but I faded out (like most 2E kids do when their acceleration needs aren't met) from feeling like there was a complete lack of 'academic challenge', and I started to question what the point of it all was.

I'd have thrived with some acceleration/extension, but instead, I endured really horrific in-class/out-of-class bullying, and eventually, going to school became too physically unsafe for me, so my dad homeschooled me.

I used to sit in class *praying* that a teacher would notice me, and see the tears welling up at the back of my eyes, and *advocate* for me by making my environment physically safe … and finding a unique way to get me into some sort of accelerated program that I'd have undoubtedly thrived in.

Ultimately, I was grade skipped, and the only benefit that had for me was one year less of school (which I *hated*, so the grade skip was welcome from this perspective, and this perspective only).

What do you wish your peers had understood about you?

I'd have loved for them to accept that yes, I was weird, but … to also ask themselves the question, 'well, what's "normal" anyway?'.

I'd have loved for them to have understood more about autism, and how it presents in autistic women. I'd have loved for them to not misunderstand my quiet introversion as being uninterested in them. (I was interested, I just found the 'loudness' and 'extroversion' of the school environment completely and utterly overwhelming.)

Additionally, I'd love to be able to thank the Year 10 girl who saw something in me and 'picked' me out of a circle I was standing on the outside of one day, and said to me 'do you want to hang out with me?' (She made the final years of my high schooling significantly less lonely, and she found my 'weirdness' completely endearing.)

What do you wish you had understood and accepted about yourself?

I didn't know I was autistic until my thirties (following my son's formal identification of his autistic culture and identity), and I *really* wish I'd known from childhood.

Everything would have made sense, and I'd have forgiven myself more, advocated for myself harder, and likely have ended up in entirely different school settings that would have been much better for my particular autistic profile.

It also would have helped when navigating parenthood in my twenties and wondering why I couldn't cope with the newborn wails. (I was in full sensory overwhelm, and I was *pumped* with anti-depressants ... and they didn't do a *thing*. I wasn't depressed;

I was in autistic meltdown and subsequent shutdown. I didn't need anti-depressants, I just needed 24–48 hours away from my babies once per quarter.)

Had I recognised my autistic culture and identity much sooner in life, I'd have had stronger friendships (on my terms), a stronger marriage (it's better now, but recognising I am autistic has played a *huge* role there), and a much better introduction to motherhood.

Life as an autistic is so much better when you know you're autistic.

What would you like this generation of autistic girls and gender diverse youth to know?

I'd like them to know that they have a plethora of role models to look to who'll constantly remind them that their autistic culture and identity is a competitive advantage, and not a list of bullet point 'deficits'.

What do you consider to be your autistic strengths?

- My ability to love people in a way they've often never been loved before
- My empathy (I feel like I drown in empathy, in all o' the right ways)
- My creative thinking
- My kindness and generosity. (I'm just not wired to hoard wealth, and I give the large majority of my 'wealth' away… because it makes me happy to do so.)

- My lack of ego, and the impact that lack of ego has on me both personally … and professionally
- My (incredibly dark) sense of humour
- My incredibly strong sense of justice, which mostly plays out as social justice (but also rears its head when I'm going up against ableist school principals on behalf of my son)

CHAPTER 3
SCHOOL – BEYOND SURVIVAL MODE

CHAPTER HIGHLIGHTS

- **Internalised autism at school:** Being a detective to better support ladybugs whose needs are often hidden. Having neuro-affirming practices in the classroom can make all the difference too!

- **Parent and teacher communication:** Two curious minds, working together collaboratively, are better than one. Oh, and don't forget that the student voice should be front and centre!

- **Transitions:** Why transitions are difficult and how we can proactively support our ladybugs.

- **Executive functioning:** Understanding that executive functioning issues have nothing to do with the student 'trying harder'.

- **Perfectionism:** Why some autistic students constantly battle with the fear of failure and not being perfect.

- **Anxiety:** Many ladybugs also present with anxiety. This anxiety can be so severe that a student is unable to speak in class or finds themselves unable to attend school some days. These students are doing the best that they can. Always.

- **The hidden curriculum:** Understanding the complexities of social dynamics is not easy. Ladybug students may need more direct explanation around peer behaviour.

- **Schooling options:** Many of our ladybugs are missing out on their education. This is why we urgently need more flexible learning options.

- **School can't:** It is not school refusal. If they could go to school, they would. And if parents could get them to school they would. Can't. Not won't. Tough love is not the answer.

We are not going to sugar-coat it. School can be tough, especially for the majority of our ladybugs who are in the traditional mainstream school setting. It can be hard for our ladybugs, their families and teachers to succeed in a system that is not designed for neurodivergent students. It is one of the most talked about topics in our community, and whilst some ladybugs may thrive in their school setting, many experience significant struggles that span throughout their schooling journey and beyond. Too many autistic girls and gender diverse students are still slipping through the net and missing out on much-needed supports at school.

In this chapter we will explore some of these more common challenges, while offering neuro-affirming suggestions for ways parents and teachers can better support our ladybugs. We will shed light on some common co-occurring conditions within our community that can impact the schooling experience, and delve into topics including social skills groups, school attendance difficulties or 'school can't', and alternative schooling options, all with the aim of bringing awareness to some of the struggles and hidden needs of autistic girls and gender diverse young people while at school.

INTERNALISED AUTISM AT SCHOOL

Within a school setting, it is not uncommon for autistic girls and gender diverse students to be more socially aware than their male peers, and as a result, to internalise and mask or camouflage their feelings and behaviours in an attempt to fit in with others. This act of internalisation may be conscious and intentional or, alternatively, an unconscious coping mechanism to hide their true self, known as adaptive morphing.[14]

One autistic adult shared their experience with masking:

'I learnt from an incredibly young age that it was easier to be who they wanted me to be. I was bullied and it felt too dangerous to be myself. So I began dismantling my autie heart and soul – hiding all the parts of me that weren't like them. I watched them and rebuilt myself through their mirrored broken pieces of them. I got so good at it, I forgot who I really was. I was so used to shape-shifting and moulding myself to be like them, that I didn't know the cost. The exhaustion and heaviness doing that every day.'

Autistic stereotypes continue to be an ongoing challenge faced by our community, especially for our ladybugs, who often display more internalised and less understood presentations of autism. We have heard so frequently from our community that the needs of those who have an internalised response at school do not come to the teacher's attention, usually due to them being less disruptive and not fitting into the stereotyped understanding of what autism actually is. It can sometimes feel like our ladybugs are invisible. As we have previously shared, we are seen as just 'shy' or 'not disruptive', and as a result, we are less likely to have the full complexity of our needs understood or met.

One autistic parent shared their frustration with their ladybug's unmet needs being overlooked for so long:

'I wish I could go back in time. Go back to the beginning of prep, with the information I now have and tell them. Make them see. Push a little harder. Not be convinced it was me, and just my overthinking. It's the same story every year, I have hope. Hope my child will have a team around them, who will see beneath the veil of their smile. Who looks beyond her shyness, and the social mask I see them wearing, getting stronger and more attached by the day. I want them to see the real version of her, but I know she will need to feel safe enough for that, and it's just not happening, not yet. And it breaks my heart. My nights are filled with worries, wondering how she is going to thrive in a world that doesn't see the real her, or know how to meet her needs.'

The internalised autistic presentation at school can show itself in several ways. It would be helpful to think of yourself as a detective. You will need to look for the clues to find the ladybugs hiding in plain sight, uncover what they may be really experiencing behind their camouflage, behind their behaviour and feelings, to truly explore what their unmet needs are. For those new to this term, unmet needs at school includes where insufficient or inadequate support is not provided or unavailable. Unmet needs for our ladybugs can be physical, emotional, psychological, relational or educational.

> *Needs are needs – even if they are invisible, hidden and hard to find, it doesn't make them any less important.*

It is equally difficult to provide a list of all potential traits of the internalised autistic experience at school, and the potential unmet needs. They are too complex and varying. We hope the following example can illustrate the experience of one of our ladybugs.

• • •

Meet Angelica: Angelica often comes home and falls into a heap. She has what's known as after-school restraint collapse, aka she loses her shit. She has been calm, 'compliant' and regulated throughout the day. Her teachers say she is 'fine'. In fact, she is pleasant, quiet and not disruptive to anyone. But at home, it is a different story. She is letting it all out. Yelling, swearing, moody and aggressive. On the surface, it looks like she is being disrespectful. Rude even. But let's look deeper. What might be going on for Angelica at school, and what could be some of her unmet needs? As neurodivergent adults, what we know from our own lived experience is, that she is probably overwhelmed. Exhausted from holding it together all day. Stressed about making friends – and trying to keep them (seen as controlling play, but there is so much more to it). She has probably been masking, trying to hide her reactions (hey, who wants to be different at that age?) to the noisy, smelly, bright classroom. She might be thinking about all the unfair things that happened that day (hello, social justice warriors) or upset about being told off (perceived rejection) for only having beige food in her lunchbox. (Many of us have restricted eating and struggle to adhere to the school's 'healthy eating' policies.) She might have sore fingernails, from biting them to the core as she has felt the need to develop stims that are perceived as being more socially acceptable. She may not know how she is feeling (interoception) or have difficulty identifying or expressing her emotions (aka alexithymia). If we are curious and open to looking below the surface, we can explore the feelings and identify what needs are not being met for Angelica, and indeed your ladybug children and students.

To the incredible, wonderful, gentle and safe teachers – thank you. Thank you for making space to truly listen and learn from neurodivergent adults. Thank you for looking beneath the surface, and truly seeing what might be going on for our ladybugs, and recognising their needs, especially when they may be going unmet. Thank you for pushing through and seeking ways to get this support. We know it can be hard, and we want to recognise how grateful we are.

To the teachers who might be further along their journey, we implore you to challenge yourself. Seek out different sources of information, question your assumptions and prior knowledge. Take the time to think about the impact of having your students' invisible needs overlooked. The impact might not be obvious now but hearing from hundreds of autistic adults – we see it. We see the trauma and impact, and it is lifelong. So please don't overlook requests for additional accommodations because your ladybug students appear to be 'fine'. Our needs may be hidden, but they are there, and together we hope to always prioritise their safety, comfort and wellbeing.

> 'It is traumatic when you do not feel safe at school. It is traumatic getting in trouble for being yourself. It is traumatic when school believes you are being intentionally naughty. It is traumatic seeing the adults in your life not believe in you. Be the person who sees neurodivergent children and help support them to not experience school trauma.' – Kristy Forbes

There are a lot of existing materials available on trauma-informed teaching, so we won't go into too much detail here, but please consider both a trauma-informed and neuro-affirming approach to all areas of your teaching and support.

We will end this topic with some sage advice from autistic teacher, Hannah Smith, @the.atypical.teacher:

'As a neurodivergent teacher, neuro-affirming teaching is about embracing the variety of strengths that all kinds of minds bring and accepting that each of them are valid and important. It means including different modes of activities and allowing choice in topics and/or expression of learning, rather than being rigid in routines and expecting all students to learn in the same ways. It looks like offering support (such as scaffolds) to all students, not just the students identified as neurodivergent. Importantly, it means accepting that learning looks different in everyone, and adapting your classroom management system to accept this. For example, students calling out contributions should be seen as enthusiasm, not disruption, and gently reminding them of the expectation to put their hand up, instead of reprimanding them in front of their peers. It looks like valuing info-dumping as knowledge and eagerness to learn. A supportive and gentle reminder of time (and then offering the student to continue sharing ideas with you at a later time, e.g., on duty) is a more neuro-affirming approach than to reprimand it as being irrelevant, inappropriate, annoying commentary. Neuro-affirming practices should be intertwined with a trauma-informed lens, so it is wholly supportive and inclusive of every student, so that neurodivergent students, whether undiagnosed or diagnosed, are able to thrive and belong.'

PARENT–TEACHER COMMUNICATION

Teamwork makes the dream work, so they say, but how often are we truly partnering together to get the best outcome for the lady-bugs in our lives? We often hear from our teacher friends, who share they are tired, burnt out and have an incredible amount of demands on their plate. They are juggling so many different things, different needs, and are just trying their best in an under-resourced environment. We appreciate that so much. Likewise, we also hear from parents who are equally burnt out, exhausted and sometimes just surviving day to day. They too are trying their best, and trying everything they can to get help for their child. There is distress from both ends. We are not going to win any peace prizes here, solving what is undoubtedly a bigger issue for another day (or book perhaps?). What we can do, is share some guidance in the hope of taking further steps towards better collaboration.

HOW CAN PARENTS APPROACH A SCHOOL AND ASK FOR HELP FOR THEIR LADYBUG?

- **Know your rights:** firstly, it is important to understand that your child has legal rights and deserves reasonable accommodations (all accommodations are reasonable to be fair). Check with your local education department to find out more information.

- **Ask for a meeting:** if you are comfortable with a meeting, ask to meet with the school (teacher, principal or wellbeing officer). Sit down and talk about what your ladybug's specific needs and supports might be.

- **Be prepared:** download our 'Supporting autistic girls and gender diverse students' resource from our website and read it. Print it out. Highlight what applies to your ladybug. You can also think about what you know about your ladybug. What are their strengths? What might be their unmet needs? Collect any reports (sensory profiles, speech or psychology reports). Think about what you might want to cover in the meeting, don't overdo it. Keep it simple. Focus on building a good relationship. When discussing your ladybug's need (and right) to have an Individual Education or Learning Plan, prepare yourself with what sort of goals you think will help your ladybug. Focus on goals that are neuro-affirming and that don't simply encourage masking.

- **Consider your own needs:** do you need a support person? Bring one. Think about what type of meeting you feel most comfortable with. You can even ask to communicate via email if that suits your needs.

- **Don't take no for an answer:** many schools will say that they do not have time, or your ladybug isn't funded and therefore they cannot provide any individualised supports. Push back and explain why you think this is important.

One parent has shared their experience with us:

> *'I was told we can't have a meeting for her because she doesn't meet the criteria. She wasn't disruptive, didn't have a language delay and was "fine". She wasn't technically funded, and I was led to believe that meant we couldn't seek out specific supports. I reached out to my local parents' group, and what a relief. I found out that under the Disability Act, my ladybug was entitled to a meeting, and more than that, an individualised plan to help her.'*

- **Bring in the big guns:** not literally, but if you are still finding it hard to meet with the school, find out who you can escalate to. Once you've exhausted all options within the school, there may be regional contacts in your local education department, local disability advocacy groups, or you can even go to your local MP! If it all gets too much, you can ask a trusted friend or allied health professional to step in and help negotiate or mediate on your behalf.

- **Safety in numbers:** if you are feeling like you can't get the support you need alone, consider starting a parenting group of neurodivergent children. Together, you can plan and help shape the culture of the school. Perhaps join the school's parent council and raise general concerns about inclusivity at a meeting. Put together a joint front, so you don't feel so alone.

HOW CAN TEACHERS APPROACH PARENTS IF THEY THINK THEIR STUDENT MIGHT BE AUTISTIC?

For our teachers, hopefully with everything you have been learning about autistic girls, women and gender diverse students, you may be wondering if some of your students may indeed be a ladybug. How you proceed with this thought will largely depend on your school policies and relationship with the family.

If you do decide to approach a family, we do suggest framing your approach in a neutral and neuro-affirming way. It is not about getting a 'diagnosis' to change or 'fix' your student in any way. Rather, it is about exploring how you can adjust your teaching, classroom and environment to better support them. Explain that it will be better if we understand how their brain works and this can be done with the help of other professionals.

Even if you do approach a family, please understand that not everyone will be open to going down that path, and that is okay. There are also many barriers to seeking a formal autism diagnosis. This is especially true for families who might have other intersectional barriers to diagnosis including those of lower socio-economic status, or migrant or First Nations groups, who might not always have the access to appropriate resources to seek support.

Even without funding or a diagnosis, there are a lot of things that you can do to help neurodivergent children that will help all children. And generally, putting neuro-affirming strategies or accommodations in place is beneficial to the entire class.

HOW SHOULD SCHOOLS ENGAGE WITH PARENTS AFTER AN INCIDENT AT SCHOOL?

It is important to use the same trauma-informed, curious, empathetic and safe tone we (hopefully) now use with students, when engaging families. This will help all parents feel safe, especially our neurodivergent parents. There may be certain situations where schools need to call families with distressing news. How it is done can make all the difference.

Consider this scenario, a student has become dysregulated and has been outwardly violent to another student during a meltdown. Once things have calmed, it is time to call the family. Which of the following two approaches feels safer?

Option 1: 'You need to come pick up your child. They were being really disruptive and violent with the other children. They are not listening, and I just need you to come get them.'

Option 2: 'We had an incident this morning, no need to worry, your child is okay, as are all the other students. But it was a serious incident, and we really need to discuss it. We have our own ideas about what happened, but we would really appreciate your input and your help to gain your child's input into what was going on for them. We don't believe at all that their behaviour was malicious, we really do believe they were overwhelmed, and we need to reduce this feeling for them, but we need your help to do that.'

The second option was provided by Autistic teacher and parent, Dr Siobhan Lamb during an excellent episode of the *Square Peg, Round Whole* podcast – we suggest searching for it and listening.[15] What a difference that approach makes. Not only is it more neuro-affirming to the student, but it is collaborative (check), curious (check), empathetic (check), and above all provides a judgement-free, safe place for parents to receive such information. And that has to be good for everyone.

Now that we have all that out of the way, following are some common areas that autistic girls and gender diverse individuals may find challenging, along with some additional support strategies that you can use to help them while they are at school.

TRANSITIONS

Although all children can struggle with transitions at school from time to time, this tends to be more common in autistic children due to many needing predictability and routines. A young person's sensitivity to transitions can be influenced by a variety of physical (are they hungry or tired?), emotional (are they feeling stressed?) and cognitive (are they in a creative mode?) factors.

For our ladybugs, the difficulties they may have with transitions might be more subtle, and therefore may not be noticed by teachers and peers. They may not have big outbursts when they are frustrated or struggling with a transition, and instead, you may see increases in their anxious behaviour, regressions, shutdowns or school refusal as coping mechanisms.

Younger children may struggle with changes in teachers or their daily routines. Not having enough time to finish something they are working on or moving from one subject to another with little warning could create significant stress. For older girls and gender diverse youth, navigating the changes and expectations that are required with different teachers and classes each day can be challenging.

There are some strategies that can be implemented within the classroom and school environment that can help autistic girls and gender diverse young people with transitions. These include:

- Make classroom learning visual and with clear context. This will help autistic students to follow along and know what is expected of them.
- Schedules in the classroom (and at home) can show students the daily and/or weekly schedule, so they know what is coming up.
- Provide verbal and visual warnings prior to transitions so that students can finish what they are doing and mentally prepare for the change.
- Tell students if you know there will be a change in their normal routine (e.g., a school assembly, a different teacher for the day or a different schedule). Also notifying the parents of autistic students can be useful, so they can help prepare their children on what is to come.
- For older children who struggle with the transition of moving classes, consider allowing them to leave the lesson a few minutes early, so that they can get to their next class free from the noise and sensory overwhelm that can come with the entire school transitioning at the same time.
- Allowing a colour-coded system for each class can be helpful. Assigning a colour to each class, so that notebooks, folders and anything else a student needs for that class are all one colour, can help to alleviate some of the stress which can come with having to change classes. A colour-coded timesheet will provide autistic students with a system they can refer to throughout the day, so they know what they need for the next class.

If a student is getting overwhelmed by transitions, allow that child the time that they need to regulate in a way that is suitable to them (e.g., stimming, break time, etc.).

EXECUTIVE FUNCTIONING

Autistic girls and gender diverse young people often have different cognitive skills that need to be recognised and accommodated while at school, with one area of particular difficulty being executive functioning. Executive functioning impacts our ladybugs' emotional regulation and impulse control, flexibility, task initiation, organisation and planning, working memory and time management. Think of it like your brain's personal assistant or air traffic controller. Sometimes things can go well, and we seem to have things under control. But at other times, it feels like our brain's PA is on strike, or the airport is overwhelmingly busy, and no matter how much we might want to, wish to, or try to, we just can't do the thing we need to do. And it is hard – because we are then adding feelings of shame, of being labelled lazy or incompetent, of not trying hard enough. Executive functioning differences can significantly impact the way autistic students learn and engage in busy school environments, and those who struggle with it will need additional guidance, understanding and most importantly, neuro-affirming support.

Similar to strategies for transitions, support for executive functioning can look like:

- Written and visual schedules and instructions that students can refer to
- Breaking tasks into smaller steps
- Providing a look at 'the big picture'. Some students may benefit from understanding reasoning or the end result.
- Regular check-ins will help ensure that an autistic student is staying on task and understands what needs to be done
- Maintaining ongoing discussions, and listening to what the student says around supports that they need to be successful. This could include strategies to stay organised, planning for projects and assignments, helping with transitions, etc.
- Acceptance – understanding that the student is trying as hard as they can.

PERFECTIONISM

It is important to note that for some ladybugs, perfectionism – the need to attain perfection in everything – can mask or compensate for challenges with executive functioning. Perfectionism can also be a masking strategy more generally. Perfectionism can often be fuelled by a fear of judgement, rejection sensitivity, and thoughts that the young person has that they are not good enough. As a result, they may feel that everything has to be perfect, so as to avoid negative attention.

It is important for parents and teachers to be aware of perfectionism and notice when the autistic young person's need for everything to be perfect begins to take over. Taking a long time to start or complete assignments or getting frustrated because things aren't 'right' could be an indication that the child is struggling with perfectionism, which is impacting their executive functioning abilities to get tasks done. This can even lead to task refusal if a child is experiencing a period of high anxiety. Mantras such as 'near enough is good enough' can help.

Near enough is good enough.

The messages of not being accepted and not feeling good enough without being perfect significantly impact our community of autistic girls and gender diverse young people. If you notice an autistic young person who may be a perfectionist, don't be afraid to ask questions, as our good friend and ambassador Ebony Birch-Hanger has suggested: ask questions such as 'why do you need to redo that piece?' 'Why are you struggling to start that assignment?' They may need support with their executive functioning in order to get started. Alternatively, they may need support in their self-esteem and encouragement that they, and the work they are doing, are enough.

ANXIETY

If there is one thing our community have told us repeatedly, it is that many of our ladybugs are presenting with anxiety while at school, especially when they are internalising and masking their feelings or natural autistic traits to fit in. The demands of school, combined with the social pressures of friendships, can leave many autistic students feeling highly anxious throughout the school day, followed by meltdowns, shutdowns or anxiety attacks once they are home.

Anxiety can look like shyness, increased stimming, mood fluctuations, disinterest, the need to leave or extreme exhaustion. For many autistic girls and gender diverse individuals, their anxiety may be hidden and therefore appear to be quite subtle. If anxiety is not addressed within the school environment, it can result in complex ongoing issues, including school avoidance and situational mutism. Working with the school to develop an anxiety care plan that incorporates flexible practices aimed at supporting each individual autistic student may help to alleviate some of the stress that is brought on by the school day.[16]

Autistic advocate Chantell Marshall, @ShyLittlePixie, shared her thoughts with us on social anxiety and situational mutism:

'Your student or child has not deliberately chosen to stop speaking. I know it can seem confusing, particularly when their ability to speak fluctuates, but I promise you, it is not a conscious decision to become mute. It is largely an automatic reaction from their nervous system (triggered by their social phobia or anxiety) which causes their throat to tighten and their vocal cords to constrict. It is quite a frightening and suffocating experience and is certainly not a pleasant occurrence for them to endure. From my heart, the most important point I wish to emphasise to parents and teachers is that if your ladybug experiences situational mutism they are far more vulnerable in a social setting than any of their peers. When they cannot speak up, this can make them an easy target for bullying or abuse, particularly if they have a quiet, sensitive nature and are unlikely to fight back. A 'model student' is not always a safe one. Even if they are not verbal, find alternative communication tools to help them express their thoughts, feelings and needs.'

I WISH MY TEACHER KNEW ...

- How good I am at masking. I was trying SO hard it hurt!

- That just because I'm quiet and well behaved, doesn't mean I'm okay and not dying on the inside

- How much I was struggling. That their 'quiet DUX' was secretly DROWNING

- How unsafe school was for me, and how much I could have achieved if I had felt safe

- That I don't always know what's wrong and how long it will be until I am READY

- That I wish you could show a visual demonstration because when you verbally tell me what to do it makes no sense

- I take longer than others to learn new skills. Please be patient with me. I don't work well under pressure

- That every sound and movement was an assault on my senses and sent me spinning into fight/flight shutdown. I couldn't learn in that environment

- I didn't get the handbook. I felt, said, and did everything in chaos. And when you told me nobody loved me, I believed you

- When I'm being chatty and disruptive, it's because I'm distracted and dysregulated, not because I'm a mischief maker, attention seeker or intentionally naughty

- I was being who I thought she wanted me to be

- I had no friends. I was so lonely

- How much energy it takes just to show up

- I know the right answer, but sometimes my brain doesn't cooperate with my mouth

- I am quiet, have an IQ of 138 and read very well, but I still struggle to complete assignments after eight hours in school

- That when she made me stand in a corner until I explained why I was rude – I had no idea what I had said that was wrong! Then I got a desk around the corner from everyone, behind the filing cabinet for the rest of the year for my 'crimes'

- That I was autistic. That my struggle to speak or make eye contact was more than just shyness

- Isolating me from my peers would not force me in her box

- I internalised the shame about my inability to self-regulate and be 'normal' in front of my peers. It wasn't a choice

- That bullying a little kid would create life-long trauma

- I was happy sitting alone during class time and I actually learnt better this way

- I'm not trying to be difficult, I'm trying to survive in a world built against me

- That I can't 'fix' my slow processing/writing speed with 'practice'

- That punishing me makes me feel worse about myself

- How desperately I wanted to be chosen for things. My arm ached from stretching my hand up so high

- That me not speaking didn't mean that I had nothing to say

- I want to, but sometimes I just can't. I'm not deliberately trying to disobey you

- That I took the hall duty job to stay inside and away from social situations

- That everyone thinks I am annoying

- How much her support not only changed my life – but saved it

- That she was my only friend, and I will always remember her

THE HIDDEN CURRICULUM

The 'hidden curriculum' incorporates aspects of the school day that sit outside the boundaries of traditional lessons but are critical to a positive experience within the school environment. These include some of the social rules and school culture that need to be navigated. Below are some areas where autistic girls and gender diverse individuals may need some additional support.

PEER RELATIONSHIPS

Peer relationships can be challenging at the best of times; however, this can be one area where our ladybugs really struggle at school.

Autistic girls and gender diverse students can find the process of navigating typical friendships with neurotypical peers difficult. They may have a huge desire to experience friendships in the same way that their peers do but can struggle to make those friendships work. Difficulties in reading body language, interpreting language and facial expressions and understanding social nuances can have an impact on their social relationships with neurotypical peers. The result of this is that many girls turn to masking as a way to fit in.

Offering autistic girls and gender diverse young people support in navigating peer relationships can help. This can include:

- Implementing social clubs during break times that adhere to their interests, which will allow for opportunities for semi-structured play and take the pressure off needing to navigate free play times in the schoolyard. Targeted social clubs also allow autistic students to interact with those who have similar interests, which can aid in widening their social circle by connecting them with peers who have a shared interest.

- Working with students to choose a classroom or playground 'buddy' who can offer support during unstructured play times, but remember, it is vital that these relationships are genuine and not forced.

- Teaching children that there are many ways of socialising and being friends – while autistic children can be empowered with direct guidance on how to join in a game, it is equally important that neurotypical children are taught that they need to be open to different ways of being friends.

- It is common for our ladybugs to connect closely with one or two friends. If one of the goals is to expand this circle, it needs to be done safely, authentically and led by the student.

- Often, our ladybugs may find it easier to connect with those who may be older or younger than them. Allowing access to all play areas on the schoolyard can help a student to find others they connect with who may not be in their class or year.

- Autistic girls and gender diverse individuals need to feel accepted and understood by their teachers, so building an authentic relationship is critical.

- Assignments involving working with peers can be a huge source of anxiety while at school. Allowing our ladybug students to work with someone they are comfortable with or looking at other accommodations, including the option of working alone, can alleviate some of the peer-related stresses.

SOCIAL SKILLS – IT'S COMPLICATED

We're going to be honest, the subject of whether or not autistic young people benefit from some sort of social skills training or support is complex and requires a nuanced discussion. We are not going to delve into this discussion here, but we will say it is important to trust your instincts. As parents, we naturally want to help our children, and this might include navigating friendships and social situations. When we see our ladybugs experiencing social exclusion, or see their desperation to make friends, it is entirely understandable that we want to do something concrete to help them. So, how do we find an approach to supporting our ladybugs in making social connections that is neuro-affirming (and protective of their autistic identity), but is also going to equip them to navigate a world that whether we like it or not is built around the expectations and preferences of the neuro-majority?

Again, trust your instincts. If groups are focusing on teaching your ladybug how to act neurotypical like their peers, (e.g., rewarding them for making eye contact or repressing their stims) this should be a red flag. Why? We know this only encourages them to mask in order to fit in. Additionally, if the groups are trying to steer your ladybug's play into a more socially acceptable way, (e.g., rewarding them when they don't line things up) this is another red flag.

If we find social skills groups for our ladybugs that are committed to being neuro-affirming and focus on helping them find their authentic selves and develop skills that align to their values, then this can be empowering. It's always a green flag when programs are focused on understanding the nuances of communication (for example, why do some groups do this when they are communicating, while others don't?). In other words, when groups teach about differences in communication, including that all communication is just as valued and important as the majority is.

Autistic speech pathologist and CEO of the Therapist Neurodiversity Collective, Julie Roberts, shares some ideas on steering skill development towards developing neuro-affirming goals. You are welcome to consider the following goals and use these with your ladybug. Here are some neuro-affirming goals:

• Building self-esteem and promoting independence

• Teaching the differences in social communication styles between autistic and non-autistic people, and validating both

• Teaching self-advocacy skills, both in social situations and for access to supports and accommodations

- Teaching our autistic students that they have control over their own bodies, including their eyes and their stims

- Empowering our ladybugs to say 'no'

- Teaching an understanding and application of social, physical and emotional boundaries

- Teaching perspective-taking – not just other's perspectives, but their own, as well – and that all perspectives have validity, including their own

- Teaching the physical sensations associated with anxiety and how to monitor and address (rather than suppress)

- Identifying emotions and the associated vocabulary in order to develop self-awareness and other-awareness

- Teaching educators and student peers about autism from a neuro-affirming model – including social interaction differences and acceptance of differences

- Teaching educators that supports, accommodations and modifications are vital to their students' success

- Teaching educators to be literal with directions, requirements and expectations and to apply them fairly, and with empathy, as well as with a firm understanding of autism

- Teaching educators about sensory needs, modifications, supports and accommodations

- Teaching all instructors, including support staff, the need for recreational or free time to be unrestricted for autistic students just the same as the other students, rather than just one more therapeutic opportunity.[17]

BULLYING

Although many of our ladybugs have a great desire to be social and to feel included, the reality is that many are at a greater risk of being bullied compared to their neurotypical peers. In a survey conducted by Yellow Ladybugs, 71 per cent of autistic girls reported experiencing verbal bullying, social exclusion, sexual and physical assaults, and property damage at school.[18]

Bullying can include social exclusion, name calling, teasing, threats, physical and verbal intimidation, manipulation and rumours. All of these forms of bullying can be perpetuated face-to-face as well as through social media.

One parent shared their experience of supporting their teen:

'She finally got an iPhone and was so excited to make some connections online. We both were not prepared for the new ways she may experience exclusion. Instead of just having to navigate the complex world of socialising at school, it now entered her *world around the clock. Classmates set up chat groups for her class and did not include her. They shared photos of her Squishmallows at school and called her a baby. And because it was online, it had a greater reach. She was devastated, and humiliated, and was hiding it from me, in case I took her phone away. It all got too much for her, and she broke down and told me. We worked together to help set up some safe boundaries, attended some cyber safety classes, talked to her teachers, but it is still such a tricky situation. I always have to be on guard for her and it worries me a lot.'*

If not addressed, bullying can have long-term detrimental effects, which can include low self-esteem, anxiety, depression and school attendance difficulties.

Another parent shared their concerns with us:

'I know they can't force people to hang out with her. I never suggested that to her school, but I do wish they would see the way those girls are treating her. It's gotten much worse as she's gotten older and enough is enough. How could they spread such nasty rumours about her? It hurt me so much when she told me they deliberately left her out, embarrassed her in front of the entire class, and relentlessly pretended she was invisible. And no one dealt with it, because it's not violent or obvious. But I know how deep it hurts, I've been there too. I was a target too, and it destroyed me from the inside out, and it's still taking me years to unpack that pain. I want her to know that this type of treatment

shouldn't be tolerated, and it's not her fault. I will walk this path with her because it took me a long time to recognise it and know it's not okay to be treated like that.'

It is also important to learn about the subtle 'covert' bullying that many of our ladybugs experience. Some of these things may be almost impossible for people outside the interpersonal interaction to identify (which is why teachers may not always understand how or why your ladybug is feeling this way). These can include more hidden, subtle or invisible situations such as:

- Withholding information, for example, not being invited to parties/events/school activities

- Indirectly encouraging other classmates to not engage with ladybugs, purposely isolating them

- Implying that the ladybug is the problem and the reason why no one wants to hang out with them

- Setting unrealistic expectations and requests on a ladybug that are outside their comfort zone and getting annoyed when they can't complete them, or giving them tasks that are demeaning

- Lying, spreading rumours, playing horrible jokes, leaving someone out on purpose, embarrassing someone in public

- Whispering, using hand gestures and weird or threatening looks, excluding or turning your back on a person, restricting where a person can sit and who they can talk to

Understand that restorative practises or traditional methods used across the whole of the school may not be suitable for students like us. We most likely will not want to face our bully to talk it out. It is not safe and can cause further damage. It might take a longer time for us to process what happened, or we may not be able to identify how we feel about it. It doesn't mean we don't need help. It doesn't mean we don't need your comfort or validations. For whatever reason, we are usually prone to being singled out. So, we will be carrying many sensitivities with each new bullying situation. Please don't assume it is us misunderstanding or misinterpreting the situation. What this teaches us is that we cannot trust our instinct. If we are brushed off or dismissed, we will lose confidence and may not feel empowered to advocate for ourselves in the future. And this is important. Self-advocacy skills will be essential to our future safety. You can read more about that in Chapter 5, which focuses on relationships.

We are made to feel that bullying is our own fault. We are told 'well, maybe if you acted more normal, you wouldn't be bullied.' – **Neurodivergent_lou**

Neurodivergent Lou, one of our favourite advocates to follow, shared this point on bullying:

> 'When autistic people report that we are being bullied, I am tired of this being justified and seen as okay. Autistic people are made to feel that bullying is our own fault. Sometimes, autistic people are told: "well, maybe if you acted more normal, you wouldn't be bullied", "If you tried to get along more with the other children, then you wouldn't be in this situation." This gives autistic people the impression that it is okay for other people to violate our boundaries, abuse and bully us, simply because we are autistic.'

This following insight from one educator certainly illustrates the power of connection. She shared this with us:

> 'Working in the school system I see it daily. I see so many children's spark and light inside them diminish and get smaller and flicker. It makes me so, so sad. If I see a little person being singled out, I always make sure I give them a little wink or love heart with my hands. The light literally leaves their eyes in those moments. It guts me and I get so angry. These moments of micro-connection make all the difference. Then I get to work fixing it for them. I will always validate their experience. This I promise.'

Here we would like to say thank you to all the incredible teachers who protect, believe and validate our ladybugs who have experienced bullying. There are so many ways teachers can help, but what we know from our lived experience is that teachers who show they authentically care, are one of the biggest protective factors for us. More specifically, it really helps when we are listened to and validated. What might seem insignificant and small to you, may be soul crushing for us.

WHAT PARENTS CAN DO

If you have found out your ladybug is being bullied, first of all: hugs. It is really hard, and sometimes this can trigger a range of emotions, and bring up our own past traumas.

Here are some additional neuro-affirming strategies to help autistic girls and gender diverse individuals with bullying while at school:

- Ensure there is a 'safe' person and place (teacher, support staff, trusted friend) they can turn to should they be bullied or excluded.

- They may need help interpreting bullying behaviour and determining whether an act was an accident or intentional, but it is critical we do not gaslight their experience.

- Due to internalisation, they may not be able or willing to articulate their feelings. Regularly check in with them, especially if you notice there is a change in their usual behaviour, or in classroom dynamics.

- They may need assistance in understanding problems that they can fix themself versus problems where they should seek help from an adult.

- Offer lunchtime structured activities, such as drama, music, art, or reading groups, that they can participate in, or provide a safe space that is open during break times for when the student is not coping in the schoolyard or needs a break from their friends.

- When a bullying situation happens, reassure the student that it is not their fault, and allow them time to process. Support them in communicating their side of the story. Consider an exemption from restorative practices if needed, as lived experience tells us that these practices can cause more harm than good for autistic students.

- Actively promote positive, inclusive attitudes through a whole-school approach by celebrating differences and reducing stigma.

SOME OTHER THINGS TO CONSIDER

Many autistic girls and gender diverse individuals experience co-occurring conditions or other forms of neurodivergence, alongside autism. These may be always present, or something that develops over time, and can have a direct impact on how a child learns. Below are some of the more common co-occurring conditions that may require additional support.

ADHD

ADHD falls under the neurodivergent umbrella, like autism. There are three types of ADHD that parents and educators need to be aware of. The first type is known as hyperactive and impulsive ADHD. This is the type of ADHD that often comes to mind when someone says 'ADHD'. Common traits include spontaneity and impulsiveness, a desire for consistent movement, difficulties with turn taking and interrupting, and being an out-of-the-box thinker full of original ideas.

The second type is known as inattentive ADHD. This type of ADHD is often seen in girls but is the hardest to detect. Traits include frequent daydreaming and becoming easily bored and distracted, but also hyperfocus. Children with inattentive ADHD may have a hard time paying attention, or may appear forgetful; however, they are also very good at noticing things others do not and may be full of creativity and imagination.

The third type of ADHD is known as combined ADHD, the most common type of ADHD. It occurs when both hyperactive and inattentive traits are experienced, which can be felt at various intensities.

There is some overlap between the strategies used within the school environment to support ADHD children and those used to support autistic children. These strategies can include:

- Encouraging movement breaks, or incorporating movement into lessons

- Writing important information and instructions down and reminding students where they can find the information, or providing other ways they can access information – videos, screenshots, etc.

- Dividing large assignments into smaller ones

- Keeping instructions clear

- Using visuals

- And, as we have previously noted when discussing executive functioning, acceptance – understanding that the student is trying their best

There are too many strategies and accommodations for ADHD to list here, so we encourage you to explore this topic further. We have a host of videos on this topic, available to watch on our YouTube channel.

PATHOLOGICAL DEMAND AVOIDANCE (PDA)

PDA, or as we prefer to call it 'Pervasive Drive for Autonomy', a term coined by autistic activist Tomlin Wilding, is the extreme avoidance of perceived or actual demands or expectations. It is generally considered to be a profile of autism. Recognition of PDA is very limited in Australia, and in some parts of the world, and the current level of awareness and support is woefully inadequate. As PDAers, we may experience extreme levels of anxiety when demands are placed on us. These demands may be real expectations, or they may be invisible and hidden to others.

Our good friend and fellow autist Kristy Forbes says:

> 'PDA tends to be a powerful inherent protective factor for a person who requires extreme autonomy. Anything that compromises the autonomy of that person escalates their anxiety to an extreme state, causing them to appear to be grasping for phenomenal amounts of control over people, places and things. We're not always consciously choosing or deciding this but following our neurological command.'

A school environment is a place that is full of demands, and our PDA ladybugs can and will struggle and become extremely anxious. The need to resist demands can often lead us to sensory overwhelm, meltdowns and shutdowns, and school can't. Even activities that we normally enjoy can be difficult to do if the activity is seen as a demand.

It is important for parents and schools to work together to develop a plan that best supports our PDA ladybugs. From our experience, the following strategies may be helpful:[19]

- Avoiding using direct demand phrases like 'you need to', 'we have to' and 'now'

- Trying to use indirect requests, for example, 'when you are done with that worksheet, could you get out your notebook?'

- Providing choices, for example, 'Would you like to read at your desk or on the floor?'

- Allowing autonomy where possible to allow us to feel more in control

- Using humour, drama, and role play (note that this doesn't always work, so use discretion here)

- Focusing on our interests (but your interest must be genuine – we will see through it if you are insincere)

- Working with us and our families to identify our triggers and recognise our signs of anxiety, so that demands can be scaled back or reduced

- Building a trusting relationship – when we know we can trust you, we are more likely to work with you (relational safety is key!)

- Being creative and flexible – what works for us one week, may not the following week – demand avoidance is tricky in that way

- Being collaborative – work with us, involve us in the process of creating our schedule, or determining what tasks we are going to complete that day

- Reducing demands – yes, we have already said this, but are saying it again because it is so important

SENSORY PROCESSING DIFFERENCES

As we discussed in the first chapter, most autistic people experience sensory processing differences, which may cause them to struggle with understanding and regulating the information that their senses are taking in.

Sensory processing can create great challenges within the learning environment. Autistic children with sensory sensitivities may struggle with school uniforms, feel overwhelmed by the noise and change of school environments, be excessively active, 'appear clumsy' and uncoordinated, struggle with smells and eating, and have difficulties knowing what is going on within their body (interoception).

Some of these challenges can be alleviated by implementing sensory accommodations for the student while they are at school.

These could include regular movement breaks (jumping works particularly well, as it enables all the sensory systems to connect with one another, which can aid in focus), allowing the use of aids such as noise-cancelling headphones or fidgets, quiet spaces, an adjustment in rules around uniforms, permission for extra toilet breaks, and letting children out of class early to avoid bustling school hallways. We strongly believe that these sorts of accommodations should be 'normalised' in the class environment, and be something available to any and all students who would benefit from them.

TWICE EXCEPTIONALITY

Twice-exceptional, or 2E, are children who display giftedness (within the top 10 per cent of the population) in one or more area, but also have one or more disability.[20] Their exceptional ability may dominate, masking some of their disability, or their disability may dominate, masking their exceptional ability, creating a challenge that results in neither the giftedness nor the disability being recognised and addressed.

Twice-exceptional students have a specific set of skills and challenges that need to be accommodated. Traditional teaching methods often do not work for these students. The challenge with these students is that they may be 'all over the place' in terms of their year level and abilities. They may, for example, be reading well above their year level, have some areas at standard, and other areas a level much lower than their peers. The consequence is that these young people may be frustrated and disengaged, with many teachers lacking the skills to help with the specific needs of these students.

If you suspect your child may be 2E, there are cognitive tests that can be done to assess this. Once confirmed, there are organisations dedicated to helping families on their 2E journey where you can get information and support.

LEARNING DISABILITIES

A learning disability is a term that encompasses several challenges with learning, most often in the areas of reading, writing, maths and problem solving. Though not part of the autism umbrella, many autistic students can also struggle with one or more learning challenges. These can include:

- **Dyslexia:** A learning disability that affects reading and language-processing skills

- **Dyscalculia:** Dyscalculia affects a person's ability to understand and interpret numbers and math facts

- **Dysgraphia:** Dysgraphia impacts a person's fine motor skills, especially handwriting

- **Dyspraxia:** Affecting motor skills, speech, and/or movements of the mouth and tongue

- **Apraxia:** Apraxia causes difficulty in motor planning to perform tasks or movements. Apraxia of speech affects the planning and movements needed to produce speech.

- **Intellectual disability:** Intellectual disability entails difficulties in problem solving, understanding complex ideas and other cognitive skills.

Trust
your instincts.
They are
usually right.

SCHOOL CAN'T

'School can't' occurs when a child becomes extremely distressed at the idea of going to school, and as a result, repeatedly misses some or all of the school day.[21] There are a number of names for it, including 'school refusal', 'school avoidance' and even 'scoliono-phobia'; however, it is important to note that when our ladybugs are in this state, they are experiencing 'school *can't*', not school *refusal*. Their inability to go to school is not a choice, and what they are feeling is real and valid. They are not being 'naughty'. If they could go to school, they would, and as parents, if you could get them to school, you would. If you are a parent experiencing this, we know that this is hard for your whole family, and though many people do not understand it, we want to reassure you that you are not alone.

One parent shared their diary entry with us, as their family travelled the school can't journey:

> *'I was told today I had to show tough love. How do those words go together? Tough and love? I still have flashbacks, to the time they ripped you from my arms. "She will be fine" they said. But you weren't. You were holding on so hard, I still remember the hole it left in my T-shirt. But that was when you were younger. And I didn't know better. I do now. You are still clinging – not to me, but the safety of your bedroom. You haven't been to school in months. I see your heaviness – you are tired, exhausted and burnt out. That masking came at a cost, and we are now picking up the pieces. And on top of that, we are getting judged for it.*

But I don't care what they think. You just couldn't go anymore. I know. I saw it. I felt it too. Yes, it's hard on all of us, but we will make it work. We will try and get through this, and strip the stress, demand-heavy ways of the past away from you. And I hope to see you again. See you basking in your glimmers and see your heart and soul healing for the first time in a long time.'

'School can't' is a very clear case of behaviour as communication; in their action of refusing school, the young person is communicating that they do not feel safe at school. The reasons behind 'school can't' are very individual. An autistic girl or gender diverse young person may refuse to go to school because they may have separation anxiety, learning difficulties, they are experiencing social problems or bullying, or the many other struggles that come with being an autistic student within a neurotypical classroom setting. For some young people the feelings they are having of being unsafe are easy to detect. At other times, these feelings are on an unconscious level, and parents and teachers may need to dig deeper to find the root cause.

We are wired for connection but trauma redirects that to protection.

Recent findings in the areas of neuroscience and neuroception have demonstrated that our body has an innate sense of when we are safe and when we are not. Chronic stress or trauma often experienced by autistic girls and gender diverse young people from masking, anxiety, bullying and exclusion can lead the autonomic nervous system to become extra sensitive and signal danger. This creates a fight, fight, freeze or fawn response (as discussed in the first chapter) and, in some children, that fear is debilitating and the result is 'school can't'.

Navigating 'school can't' is challenging, and the process of getting your child to attend school regularly may take time. For some autistic young people, it may never happen, and you may have to see alternative schooling options (see below). As a parent or caregiver of a child experiencing 'school can't', the first thing you need to do is take a breath. This is hard, and it is worth remembering that everyone in the situation is doing their best. Next, surround yourself with people who love you, and people who 'get it'. Search for respectful and neuro-affirming 'school can't' groups online. Chances are, if they are using this language ('can't' rather than 'refusal'), they are not subscribing to old models and ways of thought that will cause further trauma to your child and yourself. Listen to podcasts, read books, try to find people who get you and what you are going through, and if needed, seek professional help. 'School can't' is usually not a sprint. It is more like a marathon, so it is important to build your community.

As caregivers, be curious and explore the potential reasons your child is finding it difficult to go to school. Why might the child not be feeling safe at school? Are their needs being met while at school? Is there covert or even overt bullying going on? Is there a lack of connection with their peers or teacher? Is the environment overwhelming? The reasons why will be individual for each child. They could also change and vary depending on the day. By being curious, we open the door to understanding what the child may be feeling and going through.

Trust your instincts and trust that your child knows their limitations. Parents are often encouraged to use rewards and punishments to make their child go to school, but at what cost? The reward of an ice-cream at the end of a week of 'good attendance' is never going to address the underlying reasons for 'school can't'. The stress of going to school and having to mask can put our children at greater risk of trauma, burnout and mental health issues.

The best way for a person to feel safe again is through connection (relationships), empathy (understanding), autonomy (control) and co-regulation (trust). Listen to what your child has to say, with the goal of understanding their perspective, free of judgement. This doesn't need to be a face-to-face conversation. For example, some young people may prefer to chat via text or sharing of memes or social media content. Using statements like 'I'm hearing you', and 'I'm here for you' can help develop a feeling of safety. And remember, many autistic young people might not actually know what they are feeling and why, so it is important to show compassion and not push for an answer. They may need gentle guidance in understanding what they are feeling.

Though it may be difficult, aim for co-regulation. As discussed in our home chapter, co-regulation basically means that you want to pull your child into your calm, instead of joining their chaos. Let's look at an example to demonstrate this.

> *Invite them to share in our calm, instead of joining their chaos.*

Imagine you are running late for work for the third day in a row, you are rushing around trying to get your children ready for school, and you walk into your young person's room, and they are still asleep. You tell them they need to get up for school and they mutter 'can't'. Suddenly this is the tipping point for you. You might scream, make threats, get angry, cry or all the above.

Logically we know that threats will not work and may potentially escalate the situation. Some of us don't have the ability to stay home all the time. Some of us are neurodivergent ourselves and this sudden change in routine causes extreme distress. However, instead of exploding and creating more chaos, co-regulation is all about keeping the situation calm. It is not easy, but when we tune into this approach, we can try to catch ourselves from escalating the situation, and hopefully begin to shift back to a place of curiosity and empathy.

Whilst talking about empathy and compassion, don't forget to think about yourself as well. There are some big emotions linked with 'school can't', even for you. It is important to think about ways you can give yourself kindness and empathy. Affirmations like 'anyone would find this hard', or 'this is hard, and I am going to be gentle to myself through this process' can help. And remember, you are not alone: there is a whole community of parents of young people experiencing 'school can't' who are ready to offer their wisdom and support.

SCHOOLING OPTIONS

Sometimes, despite everyone's best efforts, mainstream school is just not the right fit for your autistic girl or gender diverse young person. Although the 'traditional' idea of schooling may provide effective educational learning opportunities, there are alternative educational settings which are equally valid and may actually benefit some of our ladybugs more. Please remember, whatever path you go down, trust your instincts. We know it can be a frustrating road, battling an education system that often feels broken and ill equipped to support neurodivergent children. This is why we are working so hard to create resources like this, although it does often feel like it is a drop in the ocean. Below is a brief description of some of these alternative schooling options.

ALTERNATIVE AND COMMUNITY SCHOOLS

Alternative schools are schools that are not bound by traditional teaching methods and curriculum found in mainstream schools, instead offering students an alternative curriculum or approach. Examples of alternative schools include Montessori schools,

Steiner schools and student-led learning programmes including the Future Schools Alliance, and schools that adopt the Integrative Learning Approach or Universal Design for Learning. Our community have also told us that local community schools are also a good fit, as they have smaller class numbers, and typically a more trauma-informed approach.

One carer shared their ladybug's experience starting at a new community school:

> 'Once again, we jump on the hope bus. But this time it feels different. I can see it in her eyes and hear it in her voice. Her heart was crying out for others to understand her. And today they did. She was exhausted, but happy. She came home and said, "Mum, there are people who are just like me". I asked her what she wished her teachers knew all along, and she said, "I just wish they took the time to get to know the real me. I never felt safe to show them, and now I hope I can."

SPECIALIST SCHOOLS

Specialist settings, or 'special' schools, are schools which provide specialised education for students with specific disability and high needs. Special schools may cater for children with intellectual disabilities, significant language delays or children who may require physical assistance for everyday care and/or children needing extensive behavioural support. Specialist or autism-specific schools are generally not considered to be a suitable option (or even open) to ladybugs with an internalised autistic presentation and without an intellectual disability or language delay. But there may be exceptions to this on an individual basis, and some of our ladybug families have found great solace in the specialist system when all other options have failed. When it comes to supporting our individual ladybugs, we believe it is important to push aside the debate about inclusive versus segregated education (for now, because this is a debate that needs to be had) and look to all the educational options that are available and offering flexibility based on individual need.

HOME SCHOOLING

Home schooling is an educational approach where students work from home to complete their education. In this model, parents may either follow predetermined achievement standards set out by an accepted home-schooling program, or develop their own program, and use this as a basis for teaching their children within the home the skills that they are required to know. This type of program offers more flexibility in how and what is learned, and many neurodivergent students have found success in learning from home when mainstream school options have not worked. Many parents who have shifted to home schooling tell us that the crucial first step, when exiting the traditional schooling system, is to allow a period of 'unschooling' or 'deschooling'. This is especially important from a trauma-recovery perspective and recognises that it may take some time before some of our ladybug students feel safe enough to re-engage with any type of learning. There are many home-schooling networks that can be a great source of support and advice for families considering this option.

VIRTUAL SCHOOLING AND DISTANCE EDUCATION

Virtual schooling and distance education programs blend several types of educational models and aim to deliver a 'virtual class-room'. Virtual learning became widespread in 2020–21 as we attempted to combat COVID-19. Although most schools have since returned to traditional mainstream learning, there are still schools that continue to offer a virtual schooling program for students, having seen how this flexible approach has benefited some students. Virtual schooling can also be found through the Distance Education programmes run in each state – we note that eligibility and the process for applying for distance education varies from state to state.

CONCLUSION

To conclude: we've got good news, and we've got bad news. Let's start with the bad: schooling might just possibly be the longest, bumpiest, most exhausting journey you ever go on together with your ladybug. You will come across systemic barriers that will frustrate and test your patience. You will surely meet many ignorant people full of assumptions about your ladybug, and even your parenting, that will push you to your limit. There will be times when you feel helpless and isolated and you wonder why things must be so hard for your family. You are probably going to face battles you never ever imagined, and unfortunately you may have to support your ladybug through challenges that have worried you since they were born: bullying, teasing, being ignored. It is all going to be there. It may ebb and flow throughout the years, and you may even feel at times that it is too much to bear. And it might be. And that is not fair. We know. We've been there.

This is where the good news comes in. We are now living in a time when so much more is known about how to better identify and support our ladybugs. Of course, there is still a long way to go, but at this point in time, we have the best chance yet to gather the experiences of our ladybug elders and share that with you, with schools and the wider community, so we can limit the issues above. We've gathered the best information, tools, strategies and shared experiences from our community, so you do not have to walk this path alone.

MINI INTERVIEW:
LAUREN MELISSA ELLZEY,
@AUTIENELLE

Growing up, what do you wish your parent/s had understood about you?

Growing up, I wish that my parents had understood that I didn't need to be like other children my age. Instead of trying to morph me into a daughter that dressed differently, a daughter that was passionate about 'normal' subjects, a daughter who laughed at what other people found funny, or a daughter that would 'go with the flow' more, I wish that my parents had spent more of my childhood fostering and appreciating my strengths and uniqueness. I spent a lot of time trying to look and act like my allistic peers. That was a lot of energy wasted, in my opinion. I often wonder what my life would have been like if my parents had been more welcoming of my uniqueness when I was child.

What do you wish your teachers had understood about you?

Throughout my school experience, I struggled to connect with my same-age peers. I was very precocious, yet I was a rule-follower. As a result, I spent a lot of time with my teachers. Their kindness and guidance were very meaningful to me. However, I wish they had thought to highlight my social differences to my parents. If my teachers had told my parents about my social differences from their educational perspective, I think I would have been more likely to receive services, counselling, and perhaps an autism diagnosis a lot sooner. I also wish that my teachers had realised that the fluorescent lights in their classroom were affecting my sensory health to such a degree that they were triggering chronic migraines. I missed half the school year once just because of small things like painful lighting.

What do you wish your peers had understood about you?

To my same-age peers in middle school and high school: I wish you understood that difference is beautiful, not something to target or shame. I still think about some of the painful misunderstandings I experienced with my same-age peers. I think, more than anything, I wish that they knew – or that they could physically experience – how awful it felt to have them call me names like 'freak', 'weirdo', 'loser', 'annoying', and worse words, both behind my back and to my face. I wish they understood the impact of that.

What do you wish you had understood and accepted about yourself?

If I could go back in time and accept something about myself, I would accept that it is okay and wonderful to be different. I wish I could have stood tall and proud of my special interests. What a beautiful adolescence I could have had if I'd spent it with just one person who liked the things I secretly liked, instead of with a handful of ever-changing friends that I had to pretend to be someone else in order to hang around.

What would you like this generation of autistic girls and gender diverse youth to know?

I would like this generation of autistic girls and gender diverse youth to know that their strengths 1) exist, and 2) are what they can build their whole life around. Even if it seems like our parents, teachers and peers all focus on our challenges, even if we find ways to push through some of our challenges, we will never build our future upon our challenges. Find out what you love, what you are strong in, and centre your self-esteem and life path on those things. Even if someone tells you that there are no jobs for your passion, you can make that passion into a job using your uniqueness, determination and creativity.

What do you consider to be your autistic strengths?

My autistic strengths include innovative thinking, having a detail-oriented perspective and being authentic and honest. I will always be proud of my honesty, and I strongly believe that autistics should never have to learn to be dishonest. In my opinion, society could learn a thing or two from autistic integrity.

CHAPTER 4

MANAGING
MENTAL HEALTH

CHAPTER HIGHLIGHTS

- **CONTENT WARNING:** In this chapter, we will discuss various complex mental health issues that face our community. This content may be distressing for some to readers. Topics include self-harm, disordered eating and suicidal ideation.

- **Autism and mental health:** Autistic girls, women and gender diverse people experience mental health issues significantly more than autistic cisgender males and the neurotypical population. We discuss the more common mental health struggles we see in our community including anxiety and depression.

- **Autistic burnout:** Autistic burnout often involves a combination of factors including autistic overwhelm, sensory overload, extreme exhaustion and possibly depressive symptoms. It is important to learn to recognise autistic burnout and to allow space for recovery.

- **Complex mental health:** The autistic community also have higher rates of complex mental health issues such as eating disorders, self-harm and suicidality. There is no easy fix for these complex issues but if parents and schools are more aware of how these may present we may be able to better identify and support our ladybugs.

- **Seeking support when in crisis:** Learning to understand warning signs and where to seek help. Try to keep the lines of communication open with your ladybug and consider taking the time to make a safety plan with your ladybug.

- **Protective factors for mental health:** Building protective measures for your ladybug is one of the most important ways of preventing a mental health crisis. Feeling connected and not alone is so important when a student and family are in crisis. Through lived experience we know that the crisis cycle can come and go like waves. Working with your health professionals, school and supports is vital.

We preface this chapter with a content warning that there will be discussion of complex mental health conditions, including OCD and eating disorders, as well as self-harm and suicidality.

You will notice an alert icon ⚠ around particularly triggering content. If you feel this discussion may trigger you, it might be best to move on to the next chapter now.

Perhaps the most important point to make at the beginning of this chapter is that autism is not a mental health condition. However, among other factors, the impact of being autistic in a predominantly neurotypical world can result in a variety of debilitating mental health conditions. In this chapter, we provide an overview of the main co-occurring mental health conditions that may affect our autistic girls and gender diverse young people and offer suggestions on how they may be supported.

It is important to identify what we know for sure. What we know with certainty is that it is important to understand what protective measures for mental health are and to introduce them as early as possible to you and your ladybug. We know this will make a profound difference to their sense of wellbeing. We know it is critical to promote a strong sense of self-acceptance, to celebrate strengths and invest in interests. We know it is key to recognise your ladybug's triggers and have trauma-informed, safe strategies. How do we know? We know through hundreds of conversations with adult ladybugs, who have walked this path before you. We've heard. We've listened. And we are sharing. And whilst no experience is the same, and everyone is different, we hope you find comfort in knowing that you are not alone.

With that in mind, let's get to the tricky, harsh and sobering reality for some of our community. Autistic women and girls experience higher rates of mental health issues[22] compared to both autistic boys and men[23] and our neurotypical peers. As we have previously explored, it is estimated that 80 per cent of autistic females remain unidentified or undiagnosed at the age of 18.[24] It also takes two to three years longer, on average, for us to be diagnosed compared to our male peers.[25] The implications of this discrepancy are significant, and make autistic girls particularly vulnerable to mental health struggles, as you will see later in this chapter. We report a higher number of psychiatric diagnoses[26] and are 33 per cent more likely to self-harm compared to our neurotypical peers.[27] Psychiatric conditions also hospitalise almost one in four autistic women by the age 25.[28] Autistic women are twice as likely as autistic men to attempt suicide.[29] And even scarier, autistic women who also have ADHD may be at particularly high risk, as one in five will attempt suicide, compared to 1 in 11 autistic/ADHD males.[30] We know it is overwhelming to read this. But together, we can unite as a community and share, learn and protect each other.

An autistic teen shared:

> 'Be someone we can trust. A safe space that we can rely on. We don't always need you to solve or fix the problem – listening and being there is sometimes enough. We also will closely watch your reaction – we might not come back to you if you over-react. We don't want to always worry you.'

ANXIETY

Anxiety seems to be a common thread linking our ladybug community. Studies have shown that anxiety is higher for our ladybugs than their autistic males peers. But we don't need studies to tell us what we already know. Many of you are probably living through this right now. So why are our ladybugs so anxious? And what type of anxiety are they experiencing?

In previous chapters, we have spoken about all the possible social, emotional and physical triggers that may be causing some of your ladybug's anxiety. It is important to identify these and work on a plan to address any of these stressors and potential unmet needs. Let's delve into some of the common reasons our ladybugs are more susceptible to anxiety.

Social demands: generally, it is commonly known that there are more social demands on girls and women, or those of us who have been socialised as female. And it starts young. How many times have we been told to smile, be nice, be friendly. Added to that, social anxiety intensifies with all the neurotypical expectations: all the gossip and small talk in the world, making eye contact, the pressure to fit in. No wonder so many of us have anxiety. We often suppress our authentic autistic selves, to fit into what the world expects of us. Then add any other intersectional lens, including BIPOC, language, poverty – you can imagine the compounding effects of these gender, neuro or cultural-based pressures on our ladybugs.

You can find some insights in the interview at the end of this chapter, but for now, autistic psychologist Sandhya Menon shares her thoughts:

> *'It was so tricky because I was a cultural minority and a neurominority. I thought the former was why I didn't fit in – try being an autistic Swiss, Indian Singaporean.'*

Suppressing our autistic traits: We've spoken about masking and camouflaging in depth during previous chapters. This is a major contributing factor to anxiety due to both the exhaustion and the loss of authentic identity that results from masking.

One autistic adult shared their experience with social anxiety:

> *'I used to sweat bullets at school. Okay, not literally, but I would be dripping wet each day, worrying about what I should say, how to say it, when to say it. Stressed, thinking about if they would judge me. Scrutinise my words. I wasn't just shy. It was quite debilitating social anxiety, and I worked so hard to hide who I was. In hindsight, that was what was causing most of my anxiety and one of the first clues that I might have been autistic.'*

Don't believe everything you think.

Late diagnosis: We have spoken at length about the impact a late diagnosis makes on our wellbeing. The anxiety of not knowing why we are different, plus internalising it and blaming ourselves can cause a never-ending loop of anxiety, overthinking, panic and pressure.

INTERNALISED ANXIETY

Internalised anxiety is also important to understand. It describes the experience of our ladybugs who internalise or hold their stress and anxiety inside. This may involve freezing up, possibly becoming non-speaking/situationally mute, or shutting down.

On a day-to-day basis, internalised anxiety is often hidden and unseen, and therefore, it can be harder to discern when a young person needs assistance. Our ladybugs often seem fine on the surface, but beneath the veneer, they may be struggling to make it through the day. You might not even notice your ladybug is anxious. Indeed, they might not know they are anxious either (remember interoception and alexithymia). On the inside they might be experiencing a rapid heart rate, excessive sweating, lightheadedness or feeling dizzy, an inability to concentrate, nausea or a sore stomach, and a feeling of dread. On the outside, there may be few signs, and these may be as subtle as biting nails or lips. There are too many examples to list, but please consider that anxiety does not always present the way we think. More complex internalised anxiety can present as racing intrusive thoughts, withdrawal, feeling disconnected from yourself and the world around you (dissociation) and extreme avoidance.

A neurodivergent parent shared their family's experience of internalised anxiety:

> 'My autistic son would express his anxiety externally – often exploding with anger and rage. I found it so different for my daughter. My daughter would implode, internalising her anxiety. She would take all her pressures and burst inwards. I found that harder to see, manage and support.'

'It is essential that we help our ladybugs learn the difference between anxious worries and autistic needs.' – *Marie Camin, autistic clinical psychologist*

Here is a very insightful perspective on anxiety from autistic clinical psychologist Marie Camin:

> 'Working with autistic kids and adults, one of the most common barriers to necessary supports that I see is medical and allied health professionals labelling minority stress and disability as "anxiety." Anxiety disorders, by definition, involve worries which are excessive and irrational. Are our ladybugs worried and afraid? Yes. Are their nervous systems lighting up like Christmas trees when they leave their safe spaces at home to attend schools where they feel unsafe, stigmatised, disabled by the environment, and overloaded with sensory information? Of course, they are.

And this is absolutely not irrational. When we validate their fear and stress and work as a system (family, allied health, school) to meet their basic human needs, this "anxiety" seems to dissipate – something which we do not see if it is an anxiety disorder. This is not to say that autistic people cannot also develop anxiety disorders; more so that it is essential that we help our ladybugs learn the difference between anxious worries and autistic needs. Worries are the things we can be brave and push through, to help our brain learn that we can cope with it better than we thought we could. Autistic needs must be validated and supported; attempting to push through, suppress our needs, or mask distress is likely to lead to poor mental health and burnout.'

TREATING ANXIETY

Knowing when to seek professional help can be really tricky. Treatment for anxiety can include psychological support to try and develop strategies to manage the anxiety as well as medication. The type and order of treatment often depends on the healthcare team. Some health professionals will choose to trial both together while others will go to psychology as a first step, adding in medication if needed. It is important to recognise that approaches that work with neurotypical children may not always work with autistic young people.

Finding the right child psychologist can take some time, and patience and resilience are needed. Experience in working with autistic girls and gender diverse young people may be the minimum essential criteria in finding a good practitioner. If you're not sure where to begin looking, try searching for recommendations of neuro-affirming practitioners in a local autistic-led group, such as Yellow Ladybugs' regional Facebook groups.

Meeting with the psychologist before an appointment with your young person is a helpful way to ascertain what their experience is and how they approach therapy. It is also beneficial to experience the clinical environment to see if there are any sensory accommodations that can be made – even better if the psychologist offers this up front. For example, can lights be dimmed, is the space open with good natural light, does the therapist offer a selection of sensory tools to help the client regulate? How will a young person feel in this space? If the therapist sends up red flags – such as talking about 'normalising' your child – or it simply does not feel like the right fit for your child or your family, be prepared to walk away.

Finding the right medication can also take some time. It can take three or more months to stabilise on a therapeutic dose and if there is no impact, then it can take a similar amount of time to reduce the dose and start again. Try to be patient through this process, because the right medication can truly be life changing.

Local autistic-led community groups can also be vital in supporting you and your child. The autistic community will have the lived experience with local support services and be able to offer lots of practical and helpful support.

One neurodivergent parent shared her ladybug's experience with getting help about her anxiety:

> 'When we first engaged with therapy for my child it was incredibly difficult for her to speak during sessions. On one occasion we sat and drew together and we discussed what particular anxieties she might have. She listed her top worries. She listed: "1. fear of a parent dying, 2. fear of family getting sick and 3. tomatoes". The therapist seemed genuinely confused but to me this made perfect sense and was entirely reasonable. The thought of eating raw tomatoes was indeed a very stressful thought for her. Sensory aversions and food restrictions are very common for many within the ND community. This is not a choice. She was told this wasn't a big problem. The size of the problem didn't match her reaction. But this invalidated her experience. To her, it was in her top 3, which included death of a parent. Dismissing her anxiety like that, just set us both back.'

Marie Camin adds this point on the power of validation:

> 'Listening to children when they tell us what is distressing for them is so important. In paediatric psychology, we are taught to be led by the child, and to validate their reality. We are told this is so important for their development and wellbeing. It's concerning, then, that this recommendation is not generalised to working with autistic kids. Telling a child that their experiences of sensory overload are irrational and out of proportion to the reality of the situation sends a clear message – whether well-intentioned or not – that they cannot trust their reality or

their body cues. This can have serious implications for developing their emotion regulation and self-advocacy skills, both of which rely on identifying important cues from our body that something needs attention.'

DEPRESSION

While occasional sadness is typical and an important feeling for our ladybugs to experience, continued and ongoing sadness may be a sign something more serious is going on. Recognising depression in our ladybugs can be difficult. It might involve teasing out the difference between their natural autistic state, what society expects of them, and actual depression. For example, what might look like social withdrawal in your ladybug, might be their preference for isolation. You might notice a sudden decline in interests, but that might just be a natural intense hyperfocus on fewer interests. Depression will be unique for everyone; however, in our experience, noticing depression, or a decline in mental health can look like:

- Rapid mood swings
- Changes in eating patterns and/or rapid weight loss or gain
- Dramatic changes in energy or sleep patterns
- Threats to themselves or others
- Isolating themselves from friends and family (more than usual)
- Withdrawing or disengaging from preferred activities (this may be subtle)
- Suicidal thoughts, statements or attempts

- Self-harm
- Statements such as 'What's the point anymore?'

We asked our community about their experience with depression, and many described autistic depression as a strong feeling of helplessness. Feeling painfully isolated, alone and worthless. Noticing an emptiness that left them feeling stuck and numb. Interestingly, many of them experienced depression between the difficult ages of 13–15 years.

One of our community members shared:

'I remember those difficult years. I just started high school. My hormones were out of whack, my body was changing, and I hated having to start a new school. Even though primary school was torture, the familiarity at least felt safer than this huge unknown. I broke my ankle the summer before high school, so lost interest in sport (my one saving grace that used to give me such an emotional release). I finally began processing all those years of primary school. The feeling of invisibility, the sense I was no one, the realisation I was just so different. I didn't know how to process that during my younger years, but for some reason it hit me like a truck. And it felt like the worst timing. It was the perfect storm brewing, with the dark clouds of depression heading my way. At first, it just felt like nothingness. Just a stronger sense of apathy, than what I was used to feeling. I didn't understand why I couldn't fit in anywhere, and why others found it so easy. I didn't know who I was, and just felt like there was no hope for me. It felt like a relentless gaping hole of loneliness.'

TREATING DEPRESSION

Firstly, it is always best to use a preventative approach with depression. It is not that we can always prevent it, but we can try and reduce the risk through protective measures. You will find some useful information on this in the final chapter – as we explore the power of autistic identity and culture in supporting wellbeing.

Once you know your ladybug may be experiencing depression, you can explore treatment options with your mental health team. Depression is commonly treated with a combination of psychologist-delivered therapies and/or medication. The most common medications used in the general population are Selective Serotonin Reuptake Inhibitors (or SSRIs). These same medications can also be used to treat anxiety. Psychologists may try aspects of Cognitive Behavioural Therapy (CBT), which is based around changing negative thought patterns. However, many autistic adults say they have found two more recently developed forms of cognitive therapy more effective – these are Acceptance and Commitment Therapy (ACT) and Dialectical Behaviour Therapy (DBT) – both of which have a mindfulness element and are based on identifying personal values and finding ways to cope with distressing thoughts. Many of us also prefer modes of therapy that are less traditional including equine, art and animal-assisted therapy, all of which, as one ladybug parent has noted, involve much less pressure to sit and talk. Whatever the case, we really suggest you seek out approaches that make your ladybug's neurodivergence central to treatment, and that are neuro-affirming (refer back to Chapter 1 on this).

We want to share a final thought from the insightful Marie Camin:

'When mental health professionals do not have an in-depth understanding of common autistic experiences, it is easy to misdiagnose depression and therefore provide ineffective therapies. Autistic people have been saying for a long time that autistic burnout looks like depression, and that typical interventions for depression can be unintentionally harmful. And finally, research has begun to back this.[31] *Another common issue I see is depression as a result of chronic stress and executive dysfunction from unidentified and unsupported ADHD. Even with anti-depressants and psychological therapy, it is difficult to treat to depression when ADHD is not supported. This is because stress is a major factor which feeds depression, and trying to keep up in school with ADHD is stressful (regardless of their academic performance).'*

Therefore, when supporting a ladybug with depression, disability supports and accommodations which reduce stress are often essential. This means that, although we are working with a mental health condition (depression), the social model of disability still applies, and the focus should be on the environment and systems just as much as on the symptoms of depression. Social support and access to neurokin (the autistic community) will also be important to bolster self-esteem. It gives your ladybugs an opportunity to see themselves represented in their community members, where their differences and challenges are normalised, and their neurotype is celebrated.

AUTISTIC BURNOUT

When it all becomes too much, when the pressures of our environment become too great, and the masking just doesn't cut it anymore, sometimes we (as autistic people) experience burnout. Often it can sneak up on us and be quite difficult to identify (thank you, alexithymia!). Feelings of complete exhaustion, overwhelm, sensory overload, needing to sleep more, finding it hard to make decisions and feeling depleted are just some of the features of burnout.

Dr Alice Nicholls, a clinical psychologist and autistic person, has developed the Autistic Burnout Symptom Checker which may be helpful.[32] Burnout includes some symptoms that are common in depression, such as tiredness and lethargy, reduced mood, social withdrawal and a lack of motivation. This overlap means burnout may not be considered by professionals who are not aware of autistic burnout.

One of the key things to know as parents and caregivers is that adding additional demands can worsen burnout. For an autistic adult, when approaching burnout, support may be needed even to make simple decisions like what to have for dinner. It is both difficult to recognise the onset of burnout and difficult to ask for help. It is also difficult for family members to be able to adapt to taking on other roles in those times as well. As a family, you may need to rethink how you do things, and make some changes to your lifestyle and family dynamics.

Supporting your ladybug through burnout can feel extra stressful when considering the school setting, where absences are often frowned upon and advocating for small changes takes a disproportionate amount of effort. Many mainstream schools do not have the needed training, understanding and empathy to support autistic girls and gender diverse young people. This puts more pressure on families and caregivers to have the answers. If attendance is costing your ladybug their mental health, and they are experiencing burnout, it might be time to release the pressures and expectations of those outside your family and do what is best for your ladybug.

One autistic student shared what her experience was like with burnout during school:

> *'It was like my mind, body and soul were experiencing a computer shutdown. It was so different to when I was depressed. This was an extremely debilitatingly exhaustion. What I used to be able to handle sensory-wise, was completely eroded. I couldn't care for myself, and stopped brushing my hair, teeth, and even lost all my words. I could barely function. I battled too long at school, governed by neurotypical expectations, and it caught up with me. The only thing that helped me get through it was chasing healing through little to no demands, deep rest, and a complete reset. I am so grateful I was given that opportunity, without any pressure to attend school. It took an entire term, but that's what I needed.'*

COMPLEX MENTAL HEALTH

OBSESSIVE COMPULSIVE DISORDER (OCD)

Untangling the ties between autism and OCD is difficult, but what we do know is that OCD is also more common in autistic people than the non-autistic community and is often experienced in conjunction with anxiety. Data suggests 17 per cent of autistic people have OCD; of course, this may be much higher when autism is so regularly overlooked, especially in women, girls and gender diverse people.[33] In addition, autistic people are twice as likely to be diagnosed with OCD later in life.[34]

One of the key features of both OCD and autism can be repetitive behaviours. For autistic people, repetitive behaviours, such as stimming and an appreciation of order and patterns, are common. However, these are not usually linked to fear, like in OCD, where the repetitive behaviours experienced are often driven by a need to reduce or control persistent, unwanted thoughts. People with OCD can also experience suicidal obsessions and can feel unsafe when alone.

Autistic advocate Ginny Grant shared her experience of OCD:

> 'The first signs appeared for me at a young age, but it wasn't until my late thirties that OCD truly took hold of me. In times of heightened stress, images would flash through my mind: disjointed parts of violent scenes. There never seemed to be a trigger; the

disturbing images would simply emerge from my subconscious in very ordinary contexts, and I would quickly stuff them back into whatever deep, dark corner of my mind they belonged. I noticed, though, that the images seemed to be coming to the forefront of my mind more frequently, until they appeared many times a day, and I began to feel unsafe in my own skin. I was also driven by numbers: threes and fives and tens. These numbers felt safer to me, and they represented the amount of times a task needed to be performed before I could feel certain that it was complete. I checked appliances and locks over and again, to ensure they were left to my satisfaction. I feared that if I did not go through these rituals, I risked an electrical fire or a home invasion. Over time, these rituals became ever more elaborate, as I tried to alleviate the anxiety that now consumed me.'

Not surprisingly, there are no specific treatment programs for OCD in autistic people. The first steps are often a diagnosis which can begin with a GP or psychologist. Treatments can include CBT and a range of medication options. One part of CBT sometimes used with neurotypical patients is exposure and response therapy, where clinicians work with the patient to develop a plan to safely be exposed to the confronting thought or situation and then be supported to make a choice not to do the behaviour. One helpful analogy is that this is like training our bodies to only respond to a fire alarm when there is an actual fire and not when the toast has burnt.

⚠ EATING DISORDERS

Food can be such a struggle for autistic people. Sensitivity towards how food looks, tastes and smells can mean we just cannot eat certain things or be around certain foods. Our society also has rules around the social requirement to sit together to eat which can be extremely difficult both for the young autistic person and their parents or caregivers who face the ongoing judgement of others. When you combine this with some of the other sensory challenges, such as super-sensitive hearing towards chewing noises, eating can become very difficult. On the other hand, for those of us who can never tell if we are hungry or full, eating can become a handy stim or way to manage the environment and try to control anxiety in social settings.

The relationship between eating disorders and autistic women, girls and gender diverse people is complex. This is because of the large rate of underdiagnosis and misdiagnosis of both autism and eating disorders. Did you know 20–30 per cent of adults with eating disorders are also autistic?[35] Research has also shown that adolescents with disordered eating at 14 years of age were more likely to have other indicators they may also be autistic.

One autistic teen shared their experience:

> 'I stopped eating, and craved the pain that came with feeling starving. My dad thought I was attention seeking. My friends thought I was being dramatic. I didn't hurt myself for any of those reasons. In fact, I didn't really know why I was – but maybe it was because I was trying to gain some control in a world that made me feel uncomfortable and unsafe.'

If you are concerned that your autistic child may be developing an eating disorder, a great place to start is the Butterfly Foundation,[36] which offers some excellent resources explaining the different types of eating disorders and provides lots of very helpful support. Alternatively, search for neurodivergent-led resources, including those created by Eating Disorders Neurodiversity Australia (EDNA).

AVOIDANT/RESTRICTIVE FOOD INTAKE DISORDER (ARFID)

ARFID is similar to anorexia nervosa with respect to restricting food intake; however, the reasons for the restriction do not usually involve distress about body shape or size. It is commonly experienced by children and adolescents and less commonly in adulthood. Children and young people with ARFID often only like very specific foods and may have little interest in food. Those with ARFID are not always underweight, depending on the small list of foods that are consumed. One of the key concerns with restrictive eating is the significant nutritional deficiency which can impact growth and development in young people. Treatment can include a variety of clinician experts including paediatricians, GPs, dieticians, speech pathologists and psychologists.

Supporting autistic kids with ARFID must be trauma-informed; that is, collaborative, child-led, and with ongoing consent from the child – including saying 'no' to foods they are not open to trying and having this boundary respected. Many interventions attempt to use exposure under the incorrect assumptions that (1) the brain can habituate to sensory aversions, and/or (2) the sensory aversions are due to irrational anxiety. This can be traumatic for kids (as you can imagine) and lead to more entrenched eating difficulties in adolescence and adulthood.

Marie Camin, our wonderful autistic psychologist, shared their personal story with ARFID below:

> 'Despite psychology being one of my strongest special interests since I was 10, the passion to become a psychologist did not come until I was 17 – when the mental health system failed me just as it failed my family before me. After four years of struggling through secondary school, flying under the radar without supports or accommodations, I finally hit autistic burnout in Year 11 and developed a severe case of ARFID. I had seen multiple health professionals, all of whom agreed I had "an atypical presentation" which "did not neatly fit any criteria", and yet I was misdiagnosed with depression and anorexia nervosa. The treatments were ineffective and traumatising, worsening my burnout

and ARFID; ultimately, I ended up in emergency and hospitalised for several weeks due to significant medical complications from malnourishment. I came out of that with PTSD, and it took 2–3 years to recover from autistic burnout. The only correspondence my mum ever received from the school was to inform her that I had automatically failed Year 12 on attendance and that they would not be refunding the school fees. My mother will tell you how distressing it was to parent me through a mental health and medical crisis. I'm sure many of you reading this will know that same fear, overwhelm, and anger at the systems that are supposed to support us. It's not a pleasant story, and yet after all of it, I have found a way to thrive. Learning about my neurotype, unmasking, shedding shame, and connecting with my autistic community has been integral to my wellbeing. And I want you to know, that I have been able to find a way to thrive because I am resilient, I self-advocate, and radically accept myself. Because my mother loved and accepted my whole autistic self from the day I was born, and taught me never to apologise for who I am. It doesn't change the system, or cure mental health conditions, but being loved and accepted unconditionally is the fiercest suit of armour.'

SELF-HARM AND SUICIDALITY

Many of the mental health conditions that are common in autistic people are also risk factors for suicidal thoughts and self-harm. Research shows that autistic people are three times more at risk for self-harm and suicide.[37]

As parents and caregivers, hearing that our beautiful young person feels so hopeless that they see the best option would be to end their life is heart breaking and frightening. For many autistic young people in this situation, it feels like the only way to solve the suffering they are experiencing. We feel angry with the system and a world that doesn't see the awesomeness in our kids and doesn't know how to support them in the way that they need. Some days we can also share the feelings of hopelessness, wondering if the education and healthcare systems, and society in general could make it any harder. Connecting with your autistic community can be life changing. Finding your people will help you as a parent or caregiver to feel less isolated – and it is also an opportunity for your ladybugs to see their neurotype represented in their community members. This can buffer them against minority stress – the stress we feel when we experience stigma from those in the majority.

Autistic young people can feel despair and may talk of a desire to end their life. Sometimes this is the frustration of trying to find a place of belonging in a world of social media and the constant expectation to be a 'certain way'. It can also be experienced in the escalation of a meltdown or burnout. While often these thoughts can be expressed without an intent to follow them through, it is hard for parents and caregivers to know when these are thoughts of understandable frustration and when they may be a more definite plan to attempt suicide or self-harm. As parents, we are encouraged to ask our young people if they are thinking about suicide. If your child indicates they are considering suicide, even without a plan, it is important to seek professional advice (see the following section on mental health crisis support).

⚠️ Self-harm is intentionally causing physical harm or pain and can be a way to express emotional distress. It can also be a way to feel some control in a world where everything seems so out of control. Signs of self-harm can include unexplained injuries, keeping the body covered and avoiding activities where areas of self-harm would be exposed. Someone who engages in self-harm may not have suicidal intent.

One parent shared with us:

> 'I found it really hard to know how to support my teen who was self-harming. I have learned, though, that it is important to let them know that I am there for them, and that I won't judge or try and control them. I also tried to remind them indirectly of all of their positive qualities. I definitely overreacted when I first found out she was harming. It is hard not to, but I wish I hadn't shown how much it impacted me, because she didn't need that on top of what she was going through. But it's complicated,

and I am an empath – and there was no rule book on how to handle things. I do wish someone told me that even though my daughter was self-harming, it didn't necessarily mean they intended to kill themselves. I panicked and went to worst case scenario – and I don't think that helped anyone. My advice is to just look after yourself and your ladybug, trust your instincts and surround yourself with safe people.'

Transitions and change can also prompt periods of self-harm, including changes at school or home. Autistic people who find it hard to recognise and express their emotions can experience higher levels of self-harm. It is really important that you do not shame a young person, or anyone, that opens up to you about self-harming behaviours. This cannot be stressed enough – when a person is self-harming there is already intense shame and sadness. If they have chosen to speak to you, please try to be as supportive as you can.

One teen shared their experience with us:

'I went through a really difficult period when I changed schools. My mum was the only one who didn't judge me, and who knew that if she forced me to stop, I might have turned to worse options. We did try alternative options: we ripped paper, punched pillows, held ice, and the biggest change was when I was able to download the app "Calm Harm" which guided me during the times I had an urge. It's a work in progress, but I've not harmed for six months now.'

If wounds are non-life threatening, then the general advice is to ensure that wounds are clean and protected. This is something you can openly discuss with your young person if needed. Leaving wound care items around the home, easily accessible by your child, will also give them an opportunity to take care of themselves without fearing judgement. Orygen has created some helpful guidelines for parents and carers which can be found at: orygen.org.au/Training/Resources/Self-harm-and-suicide-prevention

One of the most challenging things in supporting your ladybug through this is to learn to trust your instincts or gut feelings. The other extremely hard thing to do is to sit with the pain that your young person is experiencing. As parents and caregivers, we want to fix the situation and often make well-intentioned attempts that don't improve the situation. It can then be hard not to get into a cycle of blame and guilt surrounding those efforts to support our loved ones. We all do the best we can. That is all we can do.

Anyone going through this would find it difficult.

⚠ Research unfortunately shows that young autistic people are also more likely to attempt suicide.[38] Trying to support our ladybugs through their suicidality is fraught with unknowns, difficulties and heartbreaking challenges for you both. We want you to take it seriously. Suicidality isn't normal, but it is unfortunately too common in our community. As ridiculous as this sounds, it doesn't need to be terrifying. With the right tailored support, planning and guidance, you can help your ladybug through this and reduce the risks. It is important to get professional help to equip you to better identify the warning signs, so you can build your confidence to intervene in a safe and supportive way. Knowing what, how and when to say something can be challenging.

One parent shared her advice with us:

> 'Paradoxically, it can be helpful to tell your ladybug that you see their resilience. You can see how hard they are fighting to stay alive, and how desperately they're fighting to find some solution for the pain they are in. It can feel, to them, like some outside force is torturing them. It can be hard to imagine that a part of themselves is doing it, and that part doesn't have ill intentions. It can take a long time for them to reconcile with the suicidal part and do so with compassion and love, without wanting to act on those urges. It is especially hard if what they have isn't really a desire to end their own life, but rather they're being tortured by the idea they deserve to die. They may have horrible intrusive images, and it is so hard to feel like there's nothing you can do as a parent to soothe and comfort that.'

Resources on suicide prevention with an autistic lens are few and far between, but we have found The Suicide Response Project by Latrobe University.[39] This resource is autistic-informed and includes information such as myths about suicide, suicide risk factors, suicide warning signs, how to interpret warnings and risks, what to say and do, making a plan to help, and looking after yourself.

One autistic adult shared their recollection of growing up with suicidal ideation:

> 'It wasn't always a desire to die, it was more like being trapped four floors up in a burning building and knowing your only option is to jump out the window. You are jumping to escape something that is intolerable, inescapable and overwhelmingly horrifying. It's the protective part of our brains scrabbling for solutions, trying desperately to think of answers, and that's the only thing coming to mind.'

Another adult ladybug echoed this experience:

> 'I didn't want to die. I just wanted the world to stop. I wanted to hit pause on life and take a break. I was tired, broken and couldn't work out any reason to continue. I wish my parents knew that they were not responsible for my attempts. As much as they loved, supported and tried to help me, that wasn't enough. The closest thing I found to helpful was finding a DBT therapist, who helped me work out what a "life worth living" looked like for me. It also helped me realise I can be struggling with my mental health AND still find reasons to live.'

It is hard not to panic though, especially for those of us who are deep empaths, problem solvers and live life through an anxious lens.

One autistic parent shared their diary entry, during a time when they were trying to support their teen ladybug going through suicidal ideation:

> 'One of my biggest fears is playing out right in front of me, and I just feel so powerless. It's like a runaway train, speeding further away, and I am running alongside it, trying to jump on, take the wheel and stop it from crashing. But I can't. I can only see it getting further away and watch as my own exhaustion slows me down too. It's so hard to see her be in pain for so long, knowing she is hurting herself. It's even harder, as the gears have changed lately, and now we are uncovering the depths of her pain, and how much she wants out. I don't want you to die. I love you so much. I feel like I have failed you. I didn't give you the life that you needed. I feel guilty. Have I done something wrong? Can I do more? I just don't know what to do ...'

Understandably, going through these experiences will bring up a range of emotions for the entire family and can be emotionally draining. It is normal to feel emotions such as anger, panic, resentment or guilt. It doesn't make you a bad parent, sibling or family member. Notice your emotional responses and seek professional guidance, especially when you notice a decline in your own mental health. This is natural after experiencing incidents that are overwhelmingly threatening or frightening to you and your loved ones.

SEEKING SUPPORT WHEN IN CRISIS

If your child has told you they no longer want to live, or perhaps you are concerned they want to, or are trying to, harm themselves in some way, knowing what to do can be excruciatingly difficult. Defining and determining what a crisis looks like for your ladybug may take time and observation. Not every situation will be acute and require a visit to hospital, but at the same time, situations can be unpredictable and it's important to always stay prepared. This is why a safety plan (for school and home) is so important, and something we will discuss later in this section.

Many times, a crisis will arise after-hours when you might not be able to get support from your GP, clinical psychologist or psychiatrist. If you and your family have not experienced a crisis before, it may appear to sneak up on you and take you by surprise. You may find yourself wondering how to know when to call an ambulance or visit an emergency department and how to keep your child safe.

When you sense your ladybug is in a crisis, one of the first points of contact is most often one of the state-based telephone support services (listed below). The health professionals who work at these services can provide advice on what to do to support your loved one and also how to support your family. You may be asked by health professionals if you have a safety plan in place for your family. If you are experiencing your first contact with a mental health service, this can be daunting, and the feelings of parental guilt and failure can move in. A safety plan is something you can use with your family. It can include practical safety advice like using a locked box for medicines and identifying warning signs and times when a crisis may be more likely. There are also several mobile applications that people can use to develop and share safety plans with their family and loved ones.

> *There will be times they get it wrong, and you will need to advocate for what you think is right.*

As a parent, it can take some time to understand the steps that might have led to the crisis and to develop the confidence to be able to sit with the young person. Going to hospital with a young person in crisis is tough; sitting through the agonising wait to be seen and then often being sent home with what seems like unhelpful advice and no real support can be frustrating. Hospitals don't always have the beds or resources to keep you there. They may not believe your ladybug is at acute risk, which doesn't mean she is not at a high risk, but rather that they believe she is not at an immediate risk, and a stay at hospital would not be beneficial. This can be a frustrating loop, with sometimes what feels like little sense or logic. There will be times they get it wrong, and you will need to advocate for what you think is right. Even if you do not stay at the hospital (and sometimes it can be more unsafe in the wards with other teens, as crazy as that sounds), one of the positives from visiting emergency is that a change in setting and time passing can be circuit-breakers of sorts.

At other times, the crisis will pass without the need to access emergency services.

One parent shared their experience:

'I knew all the literature around the risk of suicidality and suicide attempts for autistic youth, but nothing prepared me for when my child attempted suicide. That was hard enough, but to be sent home in the middle of the night, dosed up on meds that made her groggy and compliant, without a plan, made me furious. I was told that any stay at hospital was riskier because she was a 13-year-old girl and would be put in a ward with nearly adults. The system makes no sense. Don't be afraid to knock down those doors until you get help. There is an army of people going through the same thing as you are right now. You are not alone.'

WHAT HELPS DURING A CRISIS

What we have learned from our community is that when your ladybug is in crisis, try not to ask them a lot of questions or place any demands on them. For a parent or caregiver, this can be difficult as you figure out what to do. Communicate with them on their terms. If they prefer texting, use your phone. If they prefer going for a drive to talk side-by-side, use that option. It can also be helpful to call in support for you as the carer, someone to help with other things at home while you focus on your child. Often, once things have settled, it is possible to talk and understand the trigger that caused the escalation. Learning about mental health first aid can be a way to build knowledge and confidence in how to identify and talk to someone in crisis. Mental Health First Aid Australia offer many options, and while these courses aren't specifically aimed at young autistic people, they can be helpful.[40]

A NOTE ON INVOLVING FIRST RESPONDERS DURING A CRISIS

Mental health crisis can result in some situations where you are not feeling safe, or the safety of the other members in your family may be compromised. Trying to decide if, or when, to call the police will largely depend on your own situation, comfort levels and risk factors. Having police involved can be unpredictable, at best they will provide another avenue of support when in crisis; at worst it can cause trauma.

We know how disadvantaged our culturally and linguistically diverse and BIPOC communities are, and there may be justified fear and concerns whenever police are involved.

Side note: whilst there are not a lot of studies showing the risk for our autistic CALD and BIPOC communities when interacting with police, there are certainly many harrowing stories shared[41] justifying this concern.

Having police involved in a crisis might not actually be a choice you need to make. Sometimes police are sent out when an emergency call has been placed, or a call to Lifeline, depending on the assessment of risk. This shouldn't deter you or your ladybug from using these services; we just want you to be prepared in case it happens.

One parent shared their experience:

'I was nervous when I found out police were coming to attend our home, after a particularly violent mental health crisis my ladybug was experiencing. In my day, police had little to no understanding of mental health issues and how to respond. I was genuinely surprised and grateful for their involvement. Their empathy and respect left a really positive impression for our family and made all the difference during a difficult time.'

If you think there may be ongoing police involvement, it can help to reach out to your local police station and ask to speak with their proactive police unit or youth outreach program, so you can work together to best support your ladybug.

AUSTRALIAN STATE-BASED
MENTAL HEALTH HOTLINES[42]

- **NSW:** Mental Health Line 1800 011 511
- **Victoria:** Suicide Line Victoria 1300 651 251
- **Western Australia:** Here4U 1800 437 348
- **South Australia:** Mental Health Triage Service 131 465
- **Queensland:** Mental Health Access Line 1300 64 22 55
- **Northern Territory:** Mental Health Line 1800 682 288
- **Australian Capital Territory:** Access Mental Health
  1800 629 354
- **Tasmania:** Access Mental Health Helpline 1800 322 388

AUSTRALIA WIDE

- **Lifeline** 131 114
- **Kids Help Line** 1800 551 800
- **Headspace** 1800 650 890
- **Beyond Blue** 1300 224 636

INTERNATIONAL

For those outside of Australia, please check your local services.

PROTECTIVE FACTORS FOR MENTAL HEALTH

We wanted to end this chapter on a more positive note and talk briefly about some of the protective factors for good mental health. We will speak more about this in our chapter on autistic identity and culture, but in the meantime we think the illustration on the previous page is a great visual to explain this topic. There will be undoubtably many risks our ladybugs navigate as they grow into adults. Risk and protective factors can have a powerful influence on our mental health and overall wellbeing. A risk factor is something that increases your ladybug's chances of mental health issues, for example genetic predisposition, stressful life events, trauma, bullying, isolation, etc. A protective factor may lower your ladybug's risk of developing negative mental health outcomes. For example, finding safety in comfort items, pets, good friends. Sometimes reducing the level of risk is outside of our control, but we can actively try to build up protective factors that buffer the impacts of these risks. In other words, there may be many risks we need to navigate and overcome in childhood, but finding what lifts us up, and helps propel us forward are key.

MINI INTERVIEW:
SANDHYA MENON,
ONWARDS AND UPWARDS
PSYCHOLOGY

Growing up, what do you wish your parent/s had understood about you?

I wish they knew how tiring social events were, that my panic attacks weren't a problem with my heart, that anxiety wasn't 'all in my head', that it really was okay to explore my individual identity in a fiercely interdependent culture, and that none of the ways I behaved was a reflection about their parenting.

What do you wish your teachers had understood about you?

I wish they understood that I *needed* the detail, and the detail was important to me.

I still remember sitting in on a sports talk, discussing race preparation. The presenter was talking about drinking orange juice before a race. I put my hand up, interrupting like the ADHDer I was, and asked innocently, 'Miss, does it need to have pulp or pulp free?'

She said it didn't matter, and it did. Pulp and pulp-free orange juice had considerably different textures and nutritional make-up

I imagined, and so if she was providing advice, I wanted to make sure I was following the right one. I persisted with the question. Everyone laughed; I didn't understand why. The more I persisted, the more frustrated the teacher got. I was called 'belligerent' for trying to interrupt the talk and sent away, when all I really wanted to do was listen and really absorb what she was saying.

What do you wish your peers had understood about you?

My peers always got it – or at least, I think they did. I was a highly extroverted autistic who balanced out being the centre of attention and having quiet time by myself. They never put any pressure on me to join in but would always extend the question. The combination of being socially unaware of what other people thought (or perhaps socially apathetic) and having peers who accepted my quirks was highly protective for me.

What do you wish you had understood and accepted about yourself?

Oh, I wish I knew I was autistic! So much. It would have given me a framework to understand myself so much more. I used to happy stim and I stopped myself, calling myself bimbotic (a very nineties term, I know) for flapping my hands. I am now learning after many, many years to unmask and allow myself to stim. It feels strange, but I am loving knowing this part of myself.

I was that child who was in the library at 11 years of age, researching emotions and relationships and reading *Chicken Soup for the Teenage Soul*, and vowing to be a child psychologist. I knew I was different; I just didn't understand why. I pursued psychology because I wanted to understand the human psyche and social relationships, considering it to be the more financially productive and ADHD-friendly job path of an anthropologist. Having neuro-affirmative information about autism given to me and my parents instead of having to form my own views would have been life changing.

What would you like this generation of autistic girls and gender diverse youth to know?

I want them to know that being different is okay, and that you will find your people one day but perhaps not right now. They may not be at school. You may find them online, and online friendships aren't weird. They are real and valid and honestly one of the more authentic friendships I have formed. One of my friends who I made on Tumblr became my bridesmaid on my wedding day. Hang in there, and keep your sense of self while you find your way to your community. They're going to love you, just as you are.

What do you consider to be your autistic strengths?

There are so many. I love my sense of social justice and being value-driven. It's trademark autistic to care for a particular cause and not stop until we do something to solve it or at least change the narrative. It's what led to me writing a book, and literally helping change the narrative.

I don't have high social needs so I devote my time to doing things I find fulfilling, which give me intense joy. I enjoy being highly independent and not easily swayed by the court of public opinion.

I am authentic in my approach. Autistic people say what they mean. We're the people you can count on to be honest with you. You need people like that in your life and it's one of the reasons why I think we make fantastic friends.

What do you want to share about your culture and identity?

I knew I was different, but by virtue of the colour of my skin and its makeup, by the language I spoke, or didn't speak. Masking became my language, as second nature to me as English was. Masking earned me praise for my ability to move between social groups with ease, even though it hid behind the quest for acceptance. Autism as an identity only came much later in life, because it took many, many years of peeling back what was on the outer – what was so visible to everyone else – to find my inner self.

Growing up, I knew I was different. I was from an Indian-Swiss background in Chinese-dominant Singapore, and even when I did find Indians, I wasn't 'the right kind' of Indian. Malayalees (those from Kerala, in the southern states of India) made up 0.5 per cent of the Singaporean population, and those who didn't speak the language and were mixed-race, well, very much less so.

I felt the warm after-glow of white privilege when I invited my Swiss grandmother to school one year on Grandparents' Day. The elevation of respect and social acceptance was immediate, but not long-lasting. In the dance to find acceptance in a group, I was an astute ballerina dancing between cultural groups with ease. I learnt Mandarin and watched Chinese dramas to try to blend in with the Chinese crowd, tiptoed over to the Indians where I adopted a slight head nod when I spoke, and brought up my European heritage whenever I needed to lean on it. The only place I truly belonged and didn't need to mask was with my large, mixed-race family, where the colour of your skin didn't matter as much as love and kinship.

CHAPTER 5

RELATIONSHIPS, GENDER AND SEXUALITY: THE LOWDOWN

CHAPTER HIGHLIGHTS

- **Friendships and relationships:** Understanding the vulnerabilities our ladybugs face when navigating friendships and relationships. We need to explicitly teach our ladybugs about respectful relationships.

- **Learning to set boundaries:** When building connections with others, it is important for our ladybugs to be told the benefits and protective measures that will flow from being able to set clear boundaries for themselves.

- **Sexuality:** As your ladybug gets older, it is important to find appropriate resources and education programs to explain exactly what healthy and respectful sexual relationships look like.

- **Autism and gender identity:** The autism community are more likely to also be a part of the LGBTQIA+ community. Many call this the Double Rainbow (neurodivergent and LGBTQIA+). It is important to learn about the LGBTQIA+ community so that you are prepared to support your ladybug with questions or if your ladybug identifies as part of the LGBTQIA+ community.

- **The difference between sexual identity and gender Identity:** It is important to make sure that we all understand the differences when we talk about sexual identity and gender identity.

- **How to support a young person when they come out or are questioning:** How to safeguard our ladybugs when they want to talk to us about their identity.

- **Glossary of LGBTQIA+ Terms**

As an organisation, we have long been advocating for how important it is that autistic youth, and especially girls and gender diverse autistic young people, have access to appropriately tailored information about a range of topics including sexuality, gender diversity, and education around consent and healthy relationships. At this time, we would like to provide a content warning, as this chapter does explore topics around violence and abuse.

In this chapter, we hope to provide you with some guidance about how to best support your ladybug, as they embark on their journey in all things relationships, gender and sexuality. We also want to look at the protective measures we can take in relationships to address the particular vulnerabilities that come with being a neurodivergent young person, and the positive steps we can take to empower our ladybugs. It will become clear why we must continue to educate ourselves, foster a culture of openness and continually learn from the lived experience of our autistic community. Throughout this chapter, we have incorporated a range of quotes from autistic girls and gender diverse young people sharing their lived experience of autism, gender and sexuality. To protect the participants' identity, we have not attributed these quotes. If you're keen to delve further into this subject area, we have hosted webinars on this topic, which are freely available to watch on our YouTube channel.

Whilst our advice will support all our ladybugs, we will also specifically cover our intersectional children who are both autistic and gender and/or sexually diverse. We have also included a glossary of terms, as the LGBTQIA+ and autistic communities are broad, with a wide range of experiences, and it is unlikely that we can cover every issue relating to gender and sexuality in this chapter.

Before we jump into the specific content related to our gender and sexually diverse children, we wanted to bring up the topic of consent and healthy relationships for all our ladybugs. We recently interviewed and listened to hundreds of autistic adults, who shared their stories of violence, abuse and neglect with us. The results were confronting. We found 76 per cent of our participants had experienced sexual violence with 95 per cent of violence being from someone they knew.[43] Unfortunately, our results were not unique. In one overseas study, researchers found that autistic women had nearly three times the odds of experiencing sexual abuse as those who were not autistic.[44]

Intersectional advocate Tess Moodie recently spoke at our panel, discussing these risks:

> 'Because many of us have super strong empathy, and we feel deeply, we can mistakenly assume that everyone else is the same and has good intentions. We can be really trusting, forgive easily and often we still try to see the good in people, even when they've shown us otherwise. We often don't see the red flags or even the outright abuse, so that puts us at a bit more risk. Maybe it's because we've always wanted to fit in, we might mask or hide feelings which can result in us being compliant and be people pleasers when it comes to relationships, sex and intimacy. And then there is decoding the language that our peers

will use when we're young people and it may sound something like, "If you really like me or love me, you will have sex with me," or, "Everyone has sex, what's wrong with you?". This type of language can reinforce some of those old belief systems, and we can take things quite literally, we can mistakenly believe if we don't do it then we might lose that person that we really like, or that we're not normal, if we're not doing it.'

'"Everyone has sex, what's wrong with you?" This type of language can reinforce some of those old belief systems, and we can take things quite literally, we can mistakenly believe if we don't do it then we might lose that person that we really like, or that we're not normal.' – Tess Moodie

---

We have not shared this information to alarm you. We want to alert you to the potential risks and highlight the importance of protective factors, such as explicit education and discussion on these topics. So, what can you do? Search for neuro-affirming programs that help teach and protect on topics such as boundaries, consent, healthy/unhealthy relationships and how to identify them, how to recognise abuse and family violence, and what self-advocacy and agency looks like. There isn't a lot out there, unfortunately, but you can begin by watching our video on consent and relationships on our YouTube channel.

Supporting our young people to build on their protective measures starts with open conversation. It may feel awkward at times but this open dialogue can be life changing. You can even just start by making it clear that they can talk to you, without judgement, if they want to. So much happens outside our homes but this is one action point where we, as supporting adults, can have a huge impact on our ladybugs' wellbeing and help them to understand explicitly what healthy relationships look like and how they might feel.

FRIENDSHIPS AND RELATIONSHIPS

You might be wondering when is a good time to start discussing some of these topics. The answer is, it is never too early. Discussions can be adjusted for age; for example, we can begin by introducing some concepts through exploring healthy friendships. What you and your ladybug will learn will be a great foundation for later discussions. We won't cover all aspects that you might want to cover, but have highlighted some that may be relevant for our ladybugs when navigating healthy friendships:

BOUNDARIES

Good boundaries are essential for healthy and respectful relationships. By knowing how to help your ladybug set good relationship boundaries with friends and family, you can equip them to have a stronger foundation as they enter their adult relationships. It can help to explicitly discuss the key points that differentiate healthy relationships from toxic relationships. As we have discussed, many autistic girls and gender diverse people are particularly vulnerable to bullying, coercive behaviours, exclusion and even physical abuse by peers. This is why boundaries are such an important protective factor.

There will be many ways you can impart this knowledge, including modelling healthy boundaries yourself, as well as watching TV shows and casually highlighting when someone displays a healthy boundary.

You might even want to provide and practise some healthy boundary statements, so your ladybug will have confidence when faced with a particular situation. For example, healthy boundaries in friendships can look like this:

- No, thank you, I don't want to play that game right now.
- I am not okay with you making jokes about my insecurities.
- I can't chat right now, but I can after dinner.
- That makes me uncomfortable, can you please stop?
- I don't like the way you shared the photo of me in the group chat.
- I am struggling with my own mental health right now. I don't think I can be there in the way you need right now.
- I enjoy your company, but I am feeling really overwhelmed right now and need some downtime.

TRAUMA DUMPING

Many of our ladybugs are empaths and we are often drawn to people who are either similar to us neurologically or have other relatable challenges. This can naturally provide extreme comfort, especially if there is a history of isolation and then there is a sudden rush of feeling seen and understood due to these connected experiences. However, over time, complications can arise, as one autistic teen shared:

> 'She was my first friend in high school. I felt safe because we went through similar things, and I felt so understood. But it became harder to differentiate between what was toxic, what was typical, and what was not. I got so used to her trauma dumping, that I began to absorb it as my own. Our shared trauma bonds were the only thing keeping us connected in the end, but I didn't know how to end the friendship because I was so worried, I would add to her damage.'

Relationships that are centred around these shared trauma experiences can often be intense, until they end abruptly. We have also heard how these tricky friendships can make it more difficult to make good choices.

One parent shared:

> 'My daughter joined an online community of teens who had shared depression and eating disorders. It was so good for her, until it wasn't. I was so shocked when I found their chat thread had evolved over months from bonding about how helpless and hopeless they were all feeling to the terrible conclusion to make a suicide pact together.'

This is an extreme example, and hopefully your ladybug may never come across such situations, but it is important to consider. So many of them have lost friendships quickly and often, and they may consider anything to keep and maintain that friendship, even if it does come at a cost. It might be helpful to introduce your ladybug to a wider circle, especially through shared interests, for example, joining a local drama or art club.

HOW TO SPOT HEALTHY AND UNHEALTHY RELATIONSHIPS

There are many ways we can support our ladybugs in identifying what healthy and unhealthy relationships look like. There are many resources, articles, blogs and books on this topic, although often they do not have the important autistic-informed lens. Following is an example list of green and red flags that was created by an autistic teen. You can use this as a starting point and go through it together with your ladybug to help them create their own.

Green flags

- Authentic connection – not forced or fake!
- Enjoying our preference for interest-based deep-dive conversations and not small talk
- Someone we can be ourselves with and who supports our autistic identity
- Activity that aligns with, or at least respects our sensory preferences. Some of us will be sensory-seekers and enjoy loud music and physically demanding activities like skateboarding and surfing! Others may prefer quiet, calm and gentle activities alongside their friends or family, like reading or drawing or knitting.
- Respecting our needs, for example, prior information about what is going to happen
- They make us feel good, that is, happy and content about ourselves

Red flags

- When they do not respect our boundaries, especially when these are often hard to put in place for many of us
- They make us feel like we can't be ourselves
- They tease or taunt us with our known triggers
- They make fun of our special interests or call them childish
- When they push us to do things we are not comfortable with

Finally, it is important to explicitly state to your child that if a person is crossing these non-negotiable boundaries, something needs to change, and you can help if they need it.[45] While friendship or relationship break-ups can feel scary and painful, reassure your ladybug that having fewer friendships is better than having bad relationships and that this will allow them to find someone who does respect and appreciate them. It is easier said than done though, as one parent shared:

'When my daughter was in Grade Two and had just changed schools, she began playing with a group of girls who told her she would soon get an invitation to one of their birthday parties. She was ecstatic! It was her first-ever birthday party, and being new to the school she was particularly lonely and vulnerable, and needing to make connections. The following week she told me that she was still waiting on the invitation, as she had to follow rules in order to receive it, including sitting away from them at lunchtime and doing them small favours. It was devastatingly obvious to me what their intent was. She revealed that she had been sitting alone all week, as they had obviously wanted to remove her from their social circle. Unfortunately motives and intentions may not always be positive ones, and learning how to get a gauge on that was hard for me to do as an adult, let alone her. We had to have the hard discussion that people may say one thing but mean something else or when people say something that it may not actually be true. It was hard to see her trusting spirit get a dint from that experience, but I know how important it is to show her this now, before she enters teen and adult life.'

SEXUALITY

It's important to note that when it comes to views on sexuality, we need to move far away from the common stereotype that autistic people are not interested in, or are incapable of engaging in, relationships or sex. This desexualisation occurs often in the disability community. Many autistic advocates have challenged this assertion. In reality, autistic people can be, and are, in successful and healthy sexual relationships. Likewise, it is important to also note that many autistic people do indeed identify as asexual and aromantic and may not be interested in sex at all.

As your ladybug gets older, it is essential to have the discussion we have just covered, with regards to boundaries, safety and particular vulnerabilities, for any sexual relationships they may enter into.

When discussing sex with autistic individuals, there are existing resources to assist, such as sex education guides. It is key to be honest about conversations on safe sex and what healthy relationships look like, including different relationship set-ups. For example, as we discussed earlier with red flags in friendships, it is important to identify the 'red flags' that may exist in a sexual relationships, such as power imbalances, controlling behaviour as well as lack of reciprocity, as well as the 'green flags' like feeling supported, valued, safe and balanced around that person. For some autistic individuals, having a self-made script or additional communication methods may assist when discussing consent and how to establish this when engaging in sexual activity.

Considering the sensory and emotional elements of sex in the context of the person's individual profile may also be helpful in preparing them for whether the experience will be enjoyable or safe for them. An occupational therapist may be able to assist with such issues and provide guidance on 'sensory diets' that can help with regulation.

When seeking support for your child consider the sensory processing differences, communication differences and executive functioning differences and how these may interact with understanding sex and sexual relationships. This also applies when considering how to help the autistic person navigate safe sex and the healthcare system.

What makes
you unique
makes you
amazing.

WHY LGBTQIA+?

At Yellow Ladybugs, many of our members are part of the double rainbow community (neurodivergent and LGBTQIA+). Research shows that autistic people are more likely to have non-heterosexual sexual orientations and/or be trans and gender diverse, when compared to non-autistic groups.[46]

It has been proposed that autistic people are more fluid with their sexual preferences and practices due to not being as influenced by social norms as neurotypical people. For instance, an autistic person may be more comfortable exploring their sexuality and changing descriptions like 'lesbian' or 'gay' after having had sexual or romantic experiences, than neurotypical individuals. Sexuality exists on a spectrum, and autistic individuals can have a variety of sexual, romantic, emotional and relationship orientations. For this reason, a range of orientations are discussed in this chapter.

Before we jump into identifying these, we wanted to remind you that the role of family and friends is important. What we hear from our community is that the safety and love of their family and friends provides a protective factor on their mental health and directly impacts their wellbeing. What we also hear from our community is that our LGBTQIA+ ladybugs feel different about their gender or sexuality from a young age, although it may take years before they can put a name to it. In the meantime, even if they are privately wondering about their own identity, you can help create a safe environment by openly challenging negative stereotypes or comments about being LGBTQIA+ whenever you have the opportunity.

Yellow Ladybugs ambassador and autistic advocate, Shadia Hancock, shared:

> 'Having a supportive parent to help me with discovering my gender identity helped me feel less alone and overwhelmed, especially when I was only just finding out about the non-binary community.'[47]

Mental health organisation Headspace,[48] recently shared some common stressful experiences LGBTQIA+ youth may go through. This is relevant to our ladybugs, as it may affect their wellbeing. They include:

- Feeling even more 'different' from other people around them.
- Being subjected to or witnessing homophobic bullying, whether verbal, physical or online
- Being discriminated against about their sexuality (this is against the law in Australia)
- Feeling pressure to deny or change their sexuality
- Feeling worried about 'coming out' to friends, family, fellow students or workers, along with the possibility of being rejected, isolated or having someone tell other people without your permission
- Feeling unsupported or misunderstood by friends, family, fellow students or workers and experiencing religious or cultural pressures or rejection in terms of their sexuality

These pressures can be very stressful for our ladybugs when combined with all the other social pressures of living in a neurotypical world.

AUTISM AND DIVERSE SEXUAL IDENTITY

So let us begin unpacking some types of sexuality, to give you better clarity to support your ladybug.

Asexuality includes a variety of identities, with a range of experiences related to limited or no sexual attraction. Some asexual people may experience sexual attraction in select circumstances, without or with limited sex drive, or libido; such individuals may identify as grey-asexual. Demisexual individuals only experience sexual attraction if they have a strong emotional connection to the person. Other people may vacillate between experiencing and not experiencing sexual attraction. Data suggest that asexuality occurs more often in the autistic population.[49] Discussions about asexuality are often lacking in sex education and it is not always well understood in the community.

One ladybug shared with us:

> 'I have always been confused by attraction … I thought something was wrong with me, and because asexuality is often overlooked or not spoken about, it really made me feel further ostracised … I just wish more people around me had offered explicit, open lines of communication, so I could have explored this with safe validation.'

Like asexuality, aromanticism exists on a continuum, and can include aromantic, demiromantic and grey-aromantic perspectives. Someone who is demiromantic can only experience romantic attraction if they have a strong emotional bond with the person. A grey-aromantic person is someone who falls somewhere between aromantic and romantic, wherein they experience romantic attraction, but it is challenging to define how such attraction works. Some individuals may choose to not label or further describe how their attraction works. Attraction can also be fluid and change over time.

Another ladybug told us:

> *'You do not need to have sex to know your sexuality or sexual preferences. You are allowed to experiment with your identity and make mistakes and be supported.'*

Being both neurologically and sexually diverse means being part of two minority groups, which can potentially expose autistic LGBTQIA+, or queer, individuals to more discrimination and stigma. The concept of external pressures contributing to the 'minority stress' and increased mental health issues many marginalised groups experience is gaining more recognition when discussing healthcare and supports. Such intersectionalities may make it harder to connect to like-minded individuals; for instance, encountering a fellow autistic heterosexual person or a neurotypical LGBTQIA+ individual who does not share or understand your experiences. As Hannah Gadsby remarked in her show *Nanette*, 'Where are the quiet gays supposed to go?'

One ladybug shared with us:

'As an autistic queer young person, I have two closets I felt I needed to come out of – and both were hard. Coming out for me was extra challenging, because I am autistic and already find communication and reading emotions difficult.'

When autistic people explore their sexuality, they may encounter specific issues relating to differences in sensory processing, emotional regulation and communication. Every autistic individual has a unique combination of hypersensitivities, hyposensitivities and sensory-seeking preferences. Depending on the person's profile, sexual activity can either be highly enjoyable or incredibly uncomfortable. For instance, tactile issues related to touching and bodily contact could make the experience overwhelming. Furthermore, it is known many autistic individuals have differences in interoception which, as we have explained, refers to your own awareness of feelings, emotions, internal body states and the effect of external factors on ourselves. This may pose challenges with processing internal states, such as changes in heart rate, breathing and muscular tension, key changes that occur during sexual activity.

To complicate things further, most sex education that occurs tends to centre on heterosexual experiences and is presented in a way that is more accessible for a neurotypical audience. Unfortunately, much of what exists in the school-based curriculum and references from media and popular culture may depict inaccuracies in relationships. Autistic individuals also can be excluded from discussions about sex and sex education due to support persons feeling discomfort about discussing such topics.[50]

Another ladybug shared this with us:

> *'I am [an] autistic teen and it can be hard for me to find LGBTQIA+ spaces that are safe and accessible for me – they are usually busy [and] loud places. This makes me stressed as I don't think I will find my people, and worry I won't fit in both as an autistic person and queer person.'*

AUTISM AND GENDER IDENTITY

Your ladybug may be exploring their gender identity, which can include questioning, learning, identifying and trying things on. It can look different for each individual, and may take many twists and turns, which can eventuate in them realising they are gender diverse, or maybe not. It can be scary and overwhelming as a parent when we enter a world we may not be familiar with. The important thing to note is that your support and understanding throughout this journey is critical.

Why is this so critical? Because we know autistic gender diverse individuals experience higher levels of trauma, continuing minority stress, peer rejection, bullying and discrimination, with many reporting feeling unsafe at school, as noted above.

Being autistic and gender diverse brings its own set of challenges. Healthcare professionals and family members may presume gender expressions are a result of autistic 'special interests' and rigid and obsessive thinking. Others may feel that autistic individuals with complex communication and support needs or co-occurring intellectual and learning disabilities are incapable of understanding gender and sexuality. Such assumptions can have an impact on recognising indicators of gender dysphoria and accessing gender-affirming care. It is important for professionals to realise that often autistic gender diverse individuals benefit from having both differences understood and supported during the process.

Studies have shown that 6.5 per cent of autistic adolescents and 11.4 per cent of autistic adults reported that they wished to be a gender other than what they had been assigned at birth.[51] Autism also seems to be more common among the trans and gender diverse population when compared to the general population, with approximately 5–20 per cent of people with gender dysphoria thought to have autistic traits. A theory is that social constructs may not influence autistic individuals as much as non-autistic individuals due to differences in perception, understanding and acceptance. Many autistic people can relate to feeling as outsiders due to differences in communication, sensory processing, emotional regulation and behaviour. This may make it easier for some autistic people to discover, embrace and express themselves as trans, gender diverse or gender non-conforming.

Shadia Hancock further shared this with us:

'Part of embracing my gender involved accepting that I do not see the world in a binary way, that it is okay to not be able to explain the entirety of your human experience and sit with the ambiguity rather than fight it. There are no rules when it comes to your experience of gender and the variety of gender is part of what makes the world more interesting; how boring it would be if there was no diversity!'

The research is still limited with regard to the overlap between autistic and trans identities; however, there has been increased discussion from autistic trans and gender diverse individuals about their experiences. The intersectionality of autism and gender identity has been termed 'autigender' by some autistic trans and gender diverse individuals to describe how such individuals feel the way being autistic is integrally linked to how they experience and understand gender. The terms 'gendervague', 'neurogender' and 'neuroqueer' have also been used by neurodivergent trans individuals for similar reasons. It is important to note that not all autistic people will identify with being autigender or view their autism as being connected to how they experience gender.

As with sexuality, interoceptive difficulties may impact an autistic individual's exploration of gender identity. This may make it harder to identify feelings of discomfort or dysphoria. Gender dysphoria is an experience trans and gender diverse individuals may experience, wherein a person's internal sense of self does not match their physical body or the way one is perceived by others. Not all trans people experience dysphoria or discover their identity until puberty or later in life. Some do not ever experience dysphoria. Differences in autistic individuals' sensory processing and interoception may also result in it taking time to figure things out. This may be because gender becomes less easy to ignore at puberty as individuals begin to develop secondary sex characteristics. Regardless of where a trans or gender diverse individual is on their journey of discovery, all experiences are valid.

HOW TO SUPPORT AN AUTISTIC PERSON WHO HAS COME OUT OR IS QUESTIONING

When your child, student or client 'comes out' to you or is questioning their gender or sexual identity, it is important to listen and validate their experiences; the individual in front of you is the expert in themselves. Importantly, honouring an individual's social transitioning, such as their name and pronouns, can be a protective factor for their mental health, with primary caregiver support having been identified as a key strategy for reducing suicidality in trans youth.

Reflect on the trust it takes to disclose; some individuals have been thinking about coming out for a long time. If you have further questions, it is crucial to seek advice and support for yourself with groups in Australia such as Parents of Gender Diverse Children,

Transcend and Minus18. Also remember that gender identity and sexuality may change over time and that everyone's journey will look different. This message can be helpful for individuals who may be questioning or 'coming out' with a change in pronouns, names or the like. There are no 'rules' when it comes to how we identify and express ourselves.

One autistic adult shared this with us:

> 'Being autistic, and a self-confessed "rigid thinker" and someone who craved predictability and concrete answers, I found it really hard to accept the fluid journey I was about to go through in my teens, as I questioned and explored my gender and sexuality.'

Be an ally for the autistic individual. It can be a challenge for autistic individuals to communicate their identity to others. Help with asserting their identity through the correct use of pronouns and names is one way of showing support. There are also speech therapy services available for trans and gender diverse clients that can provide voice and communication support.

If possible, finding a collaborative specialist team that recognises and understands the intersectionality of autism and LGBTQIA+ may assist the individual in receiving tailored support. There are different forms of support out there depending on the individual's needs including, but not limited to, speech therapy, occupational therapy, psychiatry, GPs, social workers, physiotherapy and psychology. If the autistic individual has an intellectual disability, learning disability or uses alternate forms of communication, it is important to provide multimodal forms of communication when discussing gender identity, sexuality and expression.

GLOSSARY

If you are interested in learning more about the distinction between gender identity, gender expression, sex, sexuality and romantic orientation, please refer to the Genderbread Person and the Gender Unicorn.

- **Queer:** Umbrella term used by people who are not heterosexual and may not identify with, or conform to, the gender binary

TERMS RELATING TO GENDER:

- **AGAB:** Assigned gender at birth
- **AFAB:** Assigned female at birth
- **AMAB:** Assigned male at birth
- **Transgender:** The term 'trans' is considered more inclusive than 'transgender'. Always respect individuals' preferences on how they refer to themselves.
- **Gender diverse:** Umbrella term for different gender identities
- **Non-binary:** Not identifying as binary 'man' or 'woman'. Trans people may also identify as non-binary.
- **Genderqueer:** Term used by those who do not fit the experiences of a 'man' or 'woman'.

- **Gender non-conforming:** Behaviours not typical of societal norms associated with assigned gender at birth.
- **Cisgender:** An individual whose personal gender identity correlates to the sex assigned at birth. You may see it written as 'cis'.
- **Agender:** People who do not identify with any gender.
- **Autigender:** Some autistic people use this term to describe their feeling that their autism influences how they experience gender identity.
- **Gendervague/neurogender:** A term used to describe the neurodivergent experience of trans and gender identities wherein gender identity cannot be separated from neurodivergence, similar to autigender.
- **Neuroqueer:** Being aware of your neurodivergent identity and queer identity, and recognising that they interact – also applies to other intersectionalities, for example, race, faith, culture, ethnicity, socioeconomic class.
- **Gender dysphoria:** When someone feels conflicted between their assigned gender at birth, the way one may be perceived by others and their internal experience of gender. Not all trans and gender diverse people experience dysphoria, and some only discover their trans identity or dysphoria during puberty or later in life. All experiences are valid.
- **Dysmorphia:** Perceived deformity or abnormality in the shape or size of a specific body part. Different to gender dysphoria.

TERMS RELATING TO SEXUALITY:

- **Asexuality (ace):** A type of sexual orientation where a person experiences little to no sexual attraction to anyone, and may not experience desire for sexual contact.
- **Aromanticism (aro):** A form of romantic orientation wherein a person has little or no romantic attraction and may have little to no desire to develop romantic relationships.
- **Polyamorous:** Consensual intimate relationships with more than one partner (non-monogamous).
- **Lesbian:** Non-men who are attracted to other non-men. People who identify as lesbian can include non-binary people, women or feminine-aligned people.
- **Gay:** Someone who is attracted to someone of the same gender
- **Bisexual:** Attraction to someone of the same gender, and other genders. This may include a variety of types of attractions and can vary depending on the individual. A bi person may be attracted to two or more genders.
- **Pansexual:** Sexual, romantic or emotional attraction towards people irrespective of gender identity.

MINI INTERVIEW:
LYRIC RIVERA,
NEURODIVERGENT REBEL

Growing up, what do you wish your parent/s had understood about you?

I always seemed so fiercely independent because I often didn't know how to ask for the help I needed. I wish my guardians had understood that I wasn't as mature as people thought I was and needed more support than I got. Though I seemed wise beyond my years in many ways and had some considerable strengths growing up, I also had weaknesses that other people took for granted.

What do you wish your teachers had understood about you?

The number one thing I wish my teachers would have understood about me was that my attention has always (and always will) look different than that of a neurotypical person who is not autistic and ADHD.

When I fidgeted, drew, failed to give eye contact and couldn't sit still in my seat, I wasn't trying to be disrespectful.

If I'm looking away, down or seem disengaged, that doesn't mean I'm not listening. Because I am a visual thinker, it is easier for me to visualise things I'm thinking of if I am not busy pretending to pay attention.

What do you wish your peers had understood about you?

I wish my peers would have been kinder to me. Growing up, other kids often bullied, teased, manipulated and picked on me. They called me names, like the R-word, twitchy, freak, weirdo, and some other choice words I won't be putting into print today.

I was a sweet kid. I wish the other kids could have truly seen me and looked past what I did that confused them, approaching me with compassion and curiosity instead of scorn.

What do you wish you had understood and accepted about yourself?

I wish I had learned to stop comparing myself to other people years ago.

When I constantly compared myself to others, it kept me in a shameful cycle, feeling insecure because I was worried about how I didn't measure up to others.

Now I try to be a better person than yesterday, always trying only to beat my personal bests.

Every person has different strengths and weaknesses, and I am no longer ashamed of mine. My one regret is not accepting those sides of myself sooner in life.

What would you like this generation of autistic girls and gender diverse youth to know?

Be yourself, whatever that looks like. Don't make yourself small to make others comfortable. Other people may not always understand you, but if you are authentic, it makes it much more likely the right people will find and love you for who you are versus who you think people want you to be.

What do you consider to be your autistic strengths?

My inability to let things go ... This tendency to get stuck on things has led me to many hobbies and passions and to master multiple skills over the years, but it is equally a gift and a curse. I get hooked on a problem, an idea or a goal, and I cannot let it go until I've reached it. This makes me a great problem solver and is excellent when the goal or problem has a solvable outcome, but can be torturous when a problem is beyond my control or power of influence.

What advice do you have for gender diverse autistic young people?

Being gender diverse isn't always easy, especially in today's world, which can be exceptionally cruel to those who are different. I know it's difficult, but try not to let the cruelty of others get you down.

Find people who support and empower you, who you feel safe around, and who empower you to be your most authentic self. Don't let other people tell you who you should be or what you want. Don't waste your time with people who expect you to be someone or something you're not.

You know yourself better than anyone outside of you can possibly know you. You know what you feel, who you are and who you want to be.

The mean and cruel people are the ones who have something wrong with them, not you. You are beautiful and wonderful just the way you are.

CHAPTER 6
EMBRACING AUTISTIC IDENTITY AND CULTURE

CHAPTER HIGHLIGHTS

- **Telling your child they are autistic:** Why it is so important for your ladybug to understand themselves and why they are valued for being exactly who they are. We explain what to consider and tips on how you can share with your ladybug that they are autistic.

- **Autistic culture:** Living life as an openly autistic individual in a way that works for your family and your ladybug can be life changing when the time is right.

- **How to develop a positive autistic identity:** There are so many valuable and exciting autistic voices. Get amongst it with your ladybug. Do your research. Ask autistic adults. Focus on the brilliant, the complex, the funny and the sparkly! A word of advice from us to you – always be careful who you follow! Avoid the doom-and-gloom narrative at all costs.

- **Exploring your own neurodivergence:** If your child has been identified as autistic it is very common to find yourself questioning your own neurotype. Our advice is to keep an open mind, be curious and seek answers if you have questions!

By this point in the book, perhaps you are beginning to feel somewhat overwhelmed. This is totally understandable. You have read a lot of information, much of which has been challenging content, particularly regarding mental health. Undoubtedly, being autistic in a neurotypical world can be problematic. However, it is so important to note that autistic girls and gender diverse young people (and indeed all autistic people) can thrive with the proper support and an outlet to be our authentic selves.

This chapter will cover some aspects of what can help your ladybug to flourish. But first, let's start at the very beginning of building a positive autistic identity – disclosing your child's 'diagnosis' to them.

TELLING YOUR CHILD THEY ARE AUTISTIC

You might wonder if telling your child that they are autistic will give them a label that will be damaging to them. However, it might help to change your mindset around this if you see it instead as unlocking a key to who they are, since this is what you are actually doing. All too often, autistic children are given incorrect labels, such as 'naughty' or 'weird' (and in the case of autistic girls 'shy' or 'bossy'). Therefore, giving them the power to say, 'Actually, I am autistic, and I was just experiencing sensory overload', can be helpful. Consequently, they can take back control over these negative labels because they understand there is no truth to them, and it is just how their brain and body work.

This conversation may feel a little daunting. You may feel a lot of pressure to get the words perfect, but it is important to stay relaxed and understand that sharing their diagnosis with them will ultimately be helpful. It may be the case that your child has started to notice they are different from their peers. Perhaps they are noticing they find specific environments or tasks more challenging. Or maybe they recognise that their interests are a little different. They may be trying to make sense of these differences and may have even started asking questions about this. If this is not the case, it likely soon will be, and it is vital to be prepared.

Whatever reason you are about to discuss their having been identified as autistic, research shows it is beneficial for them to know as early as possible. Many autistic adults have expressed the hurt that comes with not knowing sooner that they are autistic, as this has affected the way they understood themselves and the formation of their identity. Also, it is important that your child hears it from you, their most trusted person, rather than a professional.

Finding out about their autistic identity earlier may be even more important for autistic girls and gender diverse young people, many of whom often face the additional barrier and disadvantage of not representing the stereotype of what society expects autism to look like – that is, the persistent misconception that 'girls can't be autistic'. We know that these external opinions can feel invalidating. Getting to know what autistic means to your ladybug is a great protective factor to this.

One teen ladybug has shared their thoughts on what being autistic means to them:

> What does being autistic mean to me?
> It makes me unique!
> I am a born leader.
> I am a proud social justice fighter.
> I am a hyperfocus-queen.
> I have intense passions.
> I am loyal to my friends.
> I have empathy beyond compare.
> I love downtime and my own company.
> Some of my best friends are my fur babies.
> I can watch my favourite shows 100 times over.
> I am autistic and proud.

How you talk to your ladybug about their neurology can build the foundations of a positive autistic identity, so this is a meaningful conversation. However, it will be helpful to set this up as an ongoing conversation, rather than a one-off exchange. The more you discuss autism, the more it will help your child understand how their brain and body work together. This understanding can help them in so many ways, such as realising their reactions are not wrong. It also enables them to make sense of their world and empowers them to self-advocate and exercise self-compassion, which are protective factors for their mental health and wellbeing. Without this knowledge, many late-diagnosed autistic people felt broken, as if they were overreacting, failing at life and believing all the bad things they heard about themselves. You can imagine how this could be harmful and lead to mental health difficulties. This is not what we want for your child.

There is no secret script that will be entirely appropriate for every conversation. It will very much depend on your ladybug's age, cognition and curiosity. However, here are some general ideas that might help with the initial discussion:

- The most important message is that their brain works differently to most other people's brains. You do not need to overcomplicate this, and it is better to keep it simple.

- Be honest and positive. Reiterate that autism is not a disease or something that is 'wrong'. Emphasise the concept of difference. Create a family environment where difference of all kinds is celebrated.

- Personalise the conversation to them and some of the things they experience, such as 'You know how you find it hard to be in a noisy environment? That is because your sensory processing system is different, and noises can sound extra loud to you'. Making it meaningful to them will help them better process the information and make sense of it.

- Balance challenges with strengths – such as, 'this explains why you find X hard' but also 'this explains why you are so good at Y'.

- Choose to have the conversation when your child is calm, regulated and in a quiet environment with no interruptions to assist their processing.

- You may want to use visuals. You could draw two different brains and explain how even though they appear the same on the outside and have the same function, they work differently inside.

- Another common analogy that is used is that of comparing an Apple operating system to an Android one. The idea is that they both do the same things but in different ways. This might be useful for older children or teenagers, who are usually familiar with the concept. However, you could use another point of comparison of two things that are the same but have subtle differences in how they work, depending on your child's interests or age (e.g., gaming consoles).

- Encourage your child to ask questions. Many autistic children are curious and may ask in-depth biological questions. If they ask something you do not know how to answer, offer to learn the answer together, or research it for them.

- Books available can assist the conversation if your child engages well with them. An example is *The Brain Forest* by neurodivergent psychologist Sandhya Menon.

- Alternatively, some children will respond better to video content. There are many young autistic people on YouTube and social media who produce videos about all aspects of being autistic. These videos might help your ladybug to feel they are not alone and that other kids are also trying to make sense of being autistic. We recommend you watch these videos first to ensure they are suitable.

Once the initial conversation has occurred, it might take a while for your ladybug to process what it means for them and think of some questions. Ensure you give them space to do this and assure them that you will be ready to talk about it again any time in the future if they want to know more and that they can ask you anything. This is likely to be an ongoing conversation over many years, and this is completely okay!

One final note. It is important to factor in any cultural influences, when considering whether to share our autistic identity with others. Just remember, for some of us, and those particularly in the BIPOC community and other marginalised groups, there may be cultural complexities at play. This has also been discussed in Chapter 2, under the section about home life and autistic identity.

NOTES FROM OUR COMMUNITY:
AUTISTIC PRIDE MEANS ...

We asked our community what autistic pride means to them and loved their answers so much, we had to share them here.

- *Knowing I was never the problem* – *Tanna E*

- *Being able to accept myself* – *Sarina V*

- *Reassuring my inner child that I'm not broken and that my needs are valid and fully accepting myself* – *Loren J*

- *Learning to unmask and advocating unapologetically for my needs* – *Ruby W*

- *Openly, loudly celebrating our uniqueness* – *Nikki I*

- *Accepting when you need support and asking for it* – *Ella A*

- *Celebrating being autistic and how it is an integral part of who I am* – *Jacinta D*

- *Freedom* – *Sally*

- *Being part of a wonderful and uplifting community* – *Fae C*

- *Educating my peers on how fucking awesome our brains are and that it's not a scary thing – Leah L*

- *Not letting other people define us – Neurodivergent Reflections*

- *Being able to accept myself – Sarina V*

- *Finally understanding my brain more than I ever have*

- *Having the ability to have intense empathy, deep connections and a different perspective of the world than others*

- *I can help other autistics (the students) in the autism school I work at to love themselves*

- *As women we are all so creative, empathetic, quirky and we connect on a deep level*

- *Standing out when others blend in*

- *Being an example to my autistic child so they will be okay*

- *I deeply connect with animals and help shelters, including dog therapy*

- *I have a unique brain with a unique perspective on life*

- *It completes my personality*

AUTISTIC CULTURE

Autistic culture is a relatively new concept and relates to how autistic people regulate, communicate and live according to their needs to enhance their wellbeing. You may see variations to this list, but it includes things such as:

- Communication style
- No/little eye contact
- Honest and direct communication
- Deep and meaningful conversations – little desire for small talk
- Info-dumping (talking in detail about something at length)
- Tonal differences in one's voice
- Preferring text, online chat or email rather than phone or face-to-face interactions
- Alternative ways of communication, i.e., writing, AAC devices, sign language
- Black-and-white thinking
- Dressing for comfort
- Eating same or safe foods – little variety
- Buying clothing in bulk if comfortable and pleasant to wear
- Cutting out clothing tags or straps
- Wearing whatever makes a person feel happy and comfortable, no matter what people think is fashionable or age-appropriate
- Stimming
- Noise-cancelling headphones or earplugs
- Sensory tools

- Listening to the same song/artist over and over
- Watching the same TV show/film over and over
- Making the home environment calm, cosy and sensory friendly
- Routines
- A lot of screen time
- Comfort items, such as soft toys

Autistic culture adds a valuable framing for your ladybug (and yourself and your extended family, too) as it helps them understand the things that can provide them with comfort. In addition, understanding that how they are in the world is similar to many other autistic people can help them feel part of a group rather than as outsiders. The benefit of seeing autistic people as a cultural group includes shared understanding and a point of connection and relatability, which can be essential for identity development. It also helps others to understand that their preferences are not them being difficult; this is part of who they are as autistic humans. Finally, it may help you to view these behaviours through a lens of autistic culture and enable you to better understand your ladybug as a part of the wider autistic community.

It can also help you think about what adjustments you may be able to assist your ladybug with regarding the environment. We have discussed these sorts of accommodations throughout this book, but framing them in the context of autistic culture adds another layer of understanding. For example, creating an environment that is not visually overwhelming or has a quiet, calming space that the child can go to in times of stress are valuable changes. This knowledge may also enable you to become more aware of their needs and how these can fit into the family or classroom environment. For example, you could connect with them on a deeper level by immersing yourself in their world and their current focused interest, TV show or music. Showing interest in something that means a lot to them will help them to feel accepted and safe. This can help bring you closer and improve the quality of your relationship.

You may need to adjust your expectations following what you have learnt about autistic culture. Realising these small changes you can implement into your daily lives, such as encouraging your ladybug to be their authentic selves, will be very meaningful to them. If they feel they must hide part of themselves, it can be detrimental to your relationship and their self-esteem. Practising radical acceptance, where you try to understand them fully, accept them exactly how they are and show them unconditional love, is essential and can significantly strengthen your relationship.

Autistic culture is vital for young autistic people as it assists them in forming their positive autistic identity. Connecting to other autistic people through autistic culture helps to create a sense of belonging and social support, and decreases feelings of loneliness and isolation. There is a shared language and way of doing things that are accepted within this community. It can help increase self-esteem and positively impact their mental health and wellbeing, primarily as they find out other autistic people share common interests and behaviours. This greater understanding of their behaviours in the context of autistic culture enables them to correctly interpret their behaviour and empowers them to be their authentic selves. If they are misjudged inappropriately, it allows them to reframe their behaviour as an aspect of autistic culture, rather than something that is 'odd' or 'wrong'. This gives them back the power to realise they are living authentically as an autistic human. Feeling increasingly comfortable being their authentic self will have a tremendous positive impact on their identity development. They will feel a reduced need to mask as they become comfortable within this environment or with their autistic peers. Reducing the pressure to mask can positively impact the prevention of autistic burnout.

As well as being positive for your ladybug, understanding autistic culture can be important for family, friends and teachers. Autistic culture is very unlikely to be commonly known among people outside the autistic community, and you may need to explain this to others. However, this can provide a framework for them to understand your child better and accommodate their needs within different environments.

Ultimately, autistic culture opens up a range of ways for autistic individuals to better understand themselves, live authentically and experience the mental health benefits of living in this way.

Remember Kristy Forbes, our good friend and autistic power-house? She recently shared this thought with us on autistic culture:

'As a family, we continuously promote positive, neurodivergent identity in our homes and in everything that we do and understanding that the way we do life as a family is a culture. It's not deficit based, it's not disordered, it's not wrong, it's not dysfunctional. It's our autistic culture. So we do things differently because we're autistic people. It's about building up our children's sense of self, helping them to build that self-esteem, rooted in positive autistic identity. We built it up so much, that my youngest did not even realise there was an alternative view to positive autistic identity, until she went to school.'

A POSITIVE AUTISTIC IDENTITY

It may take some time for your ladybug to build a positive autistic identity.

As one autistic adult shared:

> 'It was certainly a journey to feeling positive about my autistic identity. I spent so many years using the reflection from others to form an idea of who I was. I was made to feel so defective by my peers, even with reassurance from parents. It started getting better as soon as I began feeling proud to be a little different. That planted the seed, and it grew over time. The people around me played a huge role in growing my understanding and appreciation of my autistic identity, but ultimately it was connection with my neurokin that made the biggest impact.'

Developing a positive autistic identity can be life-changing. It boosts our self-esteem and reframes our thinking to ensure we see ourselves not as failed neurotypicals but as amazing autistic people, using our strengths to do incredible things. A positive autistic identity does not suggest autistic people do not face challenges. We know many difficulties result from living in a world that is not made for us. However, focusing on our strengths, and what we are good at, helps drown out all the negative messages we receive all too often.

It is important to note that not everyone, particularly our teens, will be ready to embrace their autistic identity. For our ladybugs who have a more internalised autistic experience, masking their autism may have become a deeply ingrained and often unconscious practice. They may have been exposed to stigmatising views of autism and perceive being autistic as bad. They may feel different from their peers and be unhappy about this (even if they had been proud of their autistic identity when they were younger). They may be worried about what this means for their future. They may have trauma from teasing and bullying because of their differences. These fears are understandable, and it can be a confusing time.

Don't force or push anything onto your child. It may invalidate their feelings. If they feel uncomfortable with being autistic, or even hate it, it might be helpful to back off for now and seek further professional help. Sometimes it just takes time to process that there are some strengths to being autistic. Our ambassador, Chloe Hayden shared the following wise words at one of our conferences about her autistic identity and how to nurture that with your ladybug:

> 'Being autistic is your identity. It's not something that's attached to you. It's not something that you carry around like a handbag or a jacket that you can take off at the end of the day; it is wholeheartedly 110 per cent who you are, and that isn't a bad thing, and it doesn't have to have a negative connotation. By embracing difference, I've gotten to live every single dream and every single fairytale ending that I never, ever, ever thought that I would get to. And that wasn't in spite of my difference. And that wasn't by

trying to change myself and by trying to fit in and by trying to be someone that I knew I could never be. It wasn't by looking at the other girls in school and masking and pretending to be like them in the hopes that I would somehow magically change myself to become normal and to become neurotypical (although I did do this). It was by embracing the fact that I was autistic and by going, okay, this is who I am. What are the things that I can do that embrace the way that my mind works? And the way that my brain works is incredible. Just because something is different doesn't mean that it has to be something that's negative. I understand that being different can be really hard, especially as a teenager. Being different can suck, but once your ladybug can start to see how incredible their differences are, once they have a support group that supports those differences, and once they can start to see that in themselves, they will be so blown away with what they are capable of and what they are able to achieve.'

CONNECTING TO THE AUTISTIC COMMUNITY

One of the most powerful things you can do for your ladybug is to help them connect with other autistic people. They will likely feel a sense of belonging that they have not yet experienced, and the benefits of this are huge. Autistic people tend to have an innate understanding of each other, are accepting and non-judgemental and will take each other exactly how they are. Your ladybug won't see certain behaviours as 'weird' and will encourage people to be authentic, as they know how freeing it can be. Your ladybug will be able to make real friends who have similar expectations of friendship as they do. Loneliness can be significantly diminished by making these connections.

Connecting with the autistic community enables your ladybug to learn about their autistic strengths and autistic culture, which, as we have seen, are valuable. They can learn more about all aspects of their autism from those at a similar stage post-autism identification or those who are further along their journey and have some valuable experience to share. This is especially helpful for young people who have been identified recently and are unsure what being autistic will mean for their life. They will learn what accommodations they need and what self-advocacy skills to ask for these when necessary. It helps to ground them in the knowledge that thriving as an autistic person is possible. They can learn information about possible strategies which are likely to encourage their success.

Research has shown how crucial autistic community connection can be for autistic individuals due to the relatability, validation and feelings of being valued it brings. Another possible impact is learning to be compassionate to themselves through the consideration and kindness they offer to others in the autistic community.

Autistic people unfortunately have a long history of feeling lonely and lacking social support and a sense of belonging. Connecting to the autistic community opens up an opportunity to ensure this is not the case for your child.

It is relatively easy to find other autistic people online and through social media these days. Online peer support or special interest groups are great ways to make these connections.

In Australia, Yellow Ladybugs provides a range of interest-based activities, both online and face-to-face, for autistic girls and gender diverse young people. Our events bring our members together in inclusive, fun and sensory-friendly settings. Underpinning every Yellow Ladybugs event is our mission to foster a sense of belonging, to help our autistic members connect with their peers and to instil a sense of autistic pride. For those not able to get along to one of our events, we encourage you to find other neuro-affirming peer groups, especially if they align with your ladybug's interests!

Some therapists also run peer group sessions, often interest-based, at weekends and in school holidays, so it is worth asking if yours offers this service or knows of anything in your local area. As always, we would stress looking for groups that are neuro-affirming.

It is worth mentioning, that not everywhere you fit in is where you belong. And like any community, within the autistic space, there will be safe and unsafe people. Your ladybug may be drawn to their neuropeers; however, there are risks including trauma bonding, bullying and rejection (which can be more painful, especially when you finally feel you have found your people).

Seek out
moments of
authentic
connection.

AUTISTIC ROLE MODELS

Role models can be a powerful force to help shape the way your ladybug views themselves and makes sense of the world around them. Autistic role models can come from all areas of life including parents, older siblings, neighbours, friends, teachers, counsellors, community leaders and celebrities. Finding an autistic role model or mentor can be difficult, and just because someone is autistic, it doesn't automatically make them an ideal choice. You or your ladybug will need to consider such things as shared values, character and purpose. Begin by looking within your inner circle, to explore potential connections.

One autistic adult shared their experience with their autistic role model:

'My aunty was my autistic role model. We shared the same quirky sense of humour, dislike for small talk, and could sit side by side on our devices for hours, just stimming and chilling. She was the first person that made me truly feel good about being autistic. I could see myself in her, and it gave me such hope and confidence, knowing I too could be as content and happy as her. She really did help shape my autistic identity.'

Looking further out, you can also explore autistic role models in the public eye. Recently we have seen the meteoric rise of Yellow Ladybugs ambassador and long-time friend Chloe Hayden. Chloe is an actress, author, autistic advocate and Marie Claire Woman of the Year. Chloe is an excellent role model for young autistic people and encourages them to embrace autistic culture and celebrate their autistic identity. She has championed the phrase 'Different, not less' and encourages young autistic people to 'Find your eye sparkle', that is, to look for their strengths and talents and be proud of who they are. We really recommend checking out our joint venture, the music video 'This is me: Yellow Ladybugs', available on her YouTube channel, and her interview at the end of this chapter.

For our social justice fighters, Greta Thunberg may be a good choice. Greta is a climate change activist who took the world by storm with her impassioned pleas for increased attention on saving the environment. She is also autistic and shows how determined and focused autistic people can be if they strongly believe in a cause.

Closer to home, Grace Tame was Australian of the Year, and has talked about her autistic identity, and the challenges she has faced growing up. We also recommend our good friend Summer Farrelly, who is a young autistic advocate who is passionate about animals. You can find their accounts online.

There are many other autistic individuals who have achieved great success in their chosen careers, including Daryl Hannah (actress), Morgan Harper-Nichols (author), Susan Boyle (singer), Yellow Ladybugs ambassador Hannah Gadsby (comedian), Anne Hegarty (*The Chase*), Sandra Jones (autism researcher and academic) and Lydia X. Z. Brown (disability activist). Whilst your young person may not relate to these people due to age or generational differences, it is crucial for them to know that autistic females and gender diverse individuals can be successful in whatever chosen area they enter. You will likely find an autistic role model in almost any career your young person may be interested in pursuing. Given the right tools, autistic people can succeed in any sector.

BECOMING A SELF-ADVOCATE

It is possible that once your ladybug has acquainted themselves with the autistic community and learned about their autistic identity, they may wish to produce their own content to change the stigma around autism and help their autistic peers who are at the beginning of their journey. The drive to create change is admirable and can be beneficial for many. There are a growing number of opportunities to produce valuable content, particularly through platforms such as TikTok. However, opening themselves up to the online world can have many pitfalls, which they should consider closely. This consideration is especially important if your child is struggling with their mental health and particularly vulnerable to rejection or bullying.

If your child (and you) decide this is a direction they want to go in, ensure their security settings are high. Maybe encourage them to turn off comments and block personal messages through the apps. As you are aware, the online/social media world is a minefield for safety concerns, and it is crucial to consider these aspects. You do not want any progress on a positive autistic identity to be destroyed by ignorant and unkind trolls.

EXPLORING YOUR OWN NEURODIVERGENCE

You may have read through this book and related to much of the content. It is no secret that many parents of autistic children identify with their children's autistic identity and ultimately seek a 'diagnosis' for themselves or self-identify. Unfortunately, we are the lost generation of autistic females and gender diverse individuals, missed because of stereotypical ideas about what autism is and the flawed notion that it can only relate to males.

If you have related to anything in this book and are beginning to think you could also be autistic, you may want to explore your own neurodivergence. Many blogs, books, YouTube videos and social media accounts from late-diagnosed women and gender diverse individuals might help you discover more about their experiences. If these further confirm your suspicions, there are online tests that can give you an informal indication. (Please be aware these are not clinical diagnostic tests.) This combination may help give you the information you need regarding whether you think you are truly autistic and want to seek a formal diagnosis. For many late-diagnosed adults, this discovery is life-changing, so if you think it might be appropriate for you, we encourage you to research to see if it fits. Formal diagnosis can be lengthy and expensive, however, and it is not possible for everyone. If you cannot or do not want to seek a formal diagnosis at this stage, please be aware that self-identification is well accepted within the autistic community.

If this applies to you, we wish you good luck on your journey to self-discovery. We hope you can also embrace your positive autistic identity!

HOW TO BE A GOOD ALLY AND NURTURE A MORE INCLUSIVE WORLD

We haven't forgotten about our neurotypical friends. Allies are key, and given that you are reading this book, it seems like we are preaching to the converted, so THANK YOU! We see the effort you are making to learn more about the ladybug/s in your life and want to express how much a difference that would already be making in your journey. One of the best ways you can be a good ally is to be more inclusive and welcoming of your neurodivergent peers, students, children and clients.

Refresh yourself on the chapters where we discuss neuro-affirming language and neuro-accessibility. Continue educating yourself about what this means, as it will be ever evolving. Strive for autistic-created content (as you have so wonderfully done here) and speak out and advocate where you see injustices.

Get to know your ladybug's autistic love language! It has been fun watching our community share what their autistic love languages mean to them, including common themes such as info-dumping, parallel play, support swapping, back scratches, and finding cool random objects and giving them to us. It would be incredibly powerful, and be good allyship, if you spent the time seeking to understand what your ladybug's love language is.

Autistic author, Charli Clement, shared what their autistic love language looks like:

- Sending me gentle text reminders when I've forgotten something
- Body doubling
- Respecting boundaries
- Allowing me to info-dump
- Asking me 'let me know how I can make this less stressful'
- Making me feel safe enough to unmask
- Making sure I know I can stim
- Knowing to ask before decisions are made
- Sending me videos that remind them of me
- Picking the restaurant that has a menu online
- Swapping drinks even though I pretend I like mine
- Knowing when we should leave
- Gently encouraging me to take some time out
- Wanting me to embrace my whole self

Another way you can be a great ally is to make your office, classroom or home visibly accepting, such as having the neurodivergent flag, Yellow Ladybugs sticker or infinity symbol displayed. Going deeper, you can encourage your peers, family or colleagues to invest in training from autistic-led organisations like Yellow Ladybugs (our conferences are an incredible place to start). Lastly, take pride in their neurodivergence and always strive to help make the world more affirming and safer for your ladybug and their neurokin.

CONCLUSION

This chapter has given you some ideas to help introduce your ladybug to their autistic culture and to develop a positive autistic identity. It is important to remember we all have our own time-line; some may readily feel positive about their autistic brain, while others may take longer to accept it. Ultimately, we would love to see the next generation of autistic females and gender diverse individuals able to understand themselves better, learn how their brain and body work, make strong connections with other autistic people and possess a high level of wellbeing. Research shows that increased social support and a positive autistic identity can protect them against poor mental health. We want them to be proud of who they are and feel comfortable living authentically as the wonderful autistic human they were always born to be.

MINI INTERVIEW
CHLOE HAYDEN

Growing up, what do you wish your parent/s had understood about you?

I wish they had understood that autism isn't a scary thing, and being the parent of an autistic child is not a scary thing, either. I have always been autistic, I always will be autistic – not accepting a 'diagnosis' will not change that. Loving and supporting me for who I am, instead of the child I will never be, is the most important thing you can do for me. Focus on my strengths, my talents, my skills, and don't worry over the things that I cannot do.

What do you wish your teachers had understood about you?

The schooling system is catered to fit one kind of student, and that student will never be me. I'm not being difficult because the lights are bright and noisy and making it impossible to concentrate on anything other than the throbbing inside of my head; I'm not naughty because I'm jiggling my leg or fiddling with my pencils. I am a square peg being pushed into a circular hole. I will never fit a system that is not designed for me, and that is of no fault of my own. Have empathy, be understanding, know that not all students in your class are going to fit into this tiny system that was not created for those of us who are born to be different.

What do you wish your peers had understood about you?

Just because my mind works differently doesn't mean that I don't desperately want friends and long to be seen, heard and included. I wish they had included me. Because yes, the invitation to go out somewhere that could potentially be a sensory nightmare won't be accepted all of the time, but the invitation is still very much wanted. That way, we know we're the ones that declined an invitation, rather than never being invited in the first place.

I wish they knew to not treat me like a project. That I wasn't the 'charity case' friend, that I wasn't a community service friendship.

I wish they treated me the same way they treated all of their other friends. Because, yes, I'm different. And yes, autistic people communicate differently. And yes, understanding and leniency is important (though that should be a given with all of your friends). But at the end of the day, we're the same as everyone else, and our friendship should be too; mutually beneficial, and built on kindness and respect.

What do you wish you had understood and accepted about yourself?

I wish that I had found comfort in my autistic identity so much sooner, rather than masked and covered it up to the point of burnout and suffered from imposter syndrome for my entire teenage life. I'm an autistic human being, that's simply fact, and there is nothing wrong with that. I'm allowed to stim, I'm allowed to reach out to my support network, I'm allowed to be autistic, because I am autistic.

What would you like this generation of autistic girls and gender diverse youth to know?

Who you are is exactly who you're supposed to be. Your minds, your brains, your quirks, your youness, is all you ever need to be. Find your eye sparkles and embrace them with everything you are. Being autistic is not your hindrance, but your superpower.

What do you consider to be your autistic strengths?

I'm incredibly creative and will come up with answers to solutions that many others wouldn't because my mind hasn't been programmed to only look in the realms of seen possibilities. I'm empathetic and so incredibly passionate about social justice because there's no grey areas for me, everything is black and white, right and wrong. I want to see the good because I've been at the receiving end of the bad. In my special interests, there is no one who knows more, or is as passionate. I never hide what I'm feeling, I never say one thing while meaning another; what you see is what you get.

A FINAL THOUGHT

'We have been overlooked for many reasons including prevailing stereotypes of what autism looks like, the gender bias of standard diagnostic tools, and the way we have been socialised and viewed in our society. More generally, we know that many autistic girls and gender diverse people are being missed, or having their needs invalidated because of their more hidden or internalised autistic presentation.

The impact of this oversight extends well beyond access to diagnosis and exposes the layered vulnerabilities our community experience – including economic disadvantage, vulnerabilities to violence and abuse, and inequality in healthcare – especially in the realm of mental health, restricted access to education and limited access to communities and their autistic peers.

Thank you for hearing our war cry. To our neurodivergent community, thank you for joining us. To our allies, we invite you to stand by our side. Together, let's unite and spread these messages. For this will be our uprising, and we will indeed change the world. But for now, know that you are enough. We are enough.'

Katie Koullas
CEO, Yellow Ladybugs

ACKNOWLEDGEMENTS

We extend our thanks to:

- Meg Berryman
- Marie Camin
- Charli Clement
- Cherie Clonan
- Annie Crowe
- Allison Davies
- Lauren Melissa Ellzey
- Rebecca Gannon
- Ginny Grant
- Ebony Birch-Hanger
- Em Hammond
- Shadia Hancock
- Chloe Hayden
- Green Hill Publishing
- Emma Jacques
- Kristy Forbes
- Katie Koullas
- Dr Siobhan Lamb
- Vanessa Makropoulos
- Chantell Marshall
- Gilly McKeown
- Sandhya Menon
- Alisa Mlakar
- Tess Moodie
- JayJay Mudridge
- Chenai Mupotsa-Russell
- Neurodivergent Lou
- Natasha Staheli
- Lyric Rivera
- Julie Roberts
- Jodie Simpson
- Hannah Smith
- Dr Alberto Veloso
- Sonny Jane Wise

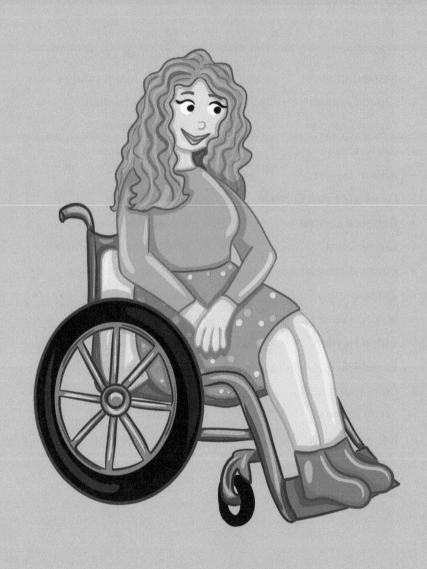

ENDNOTES

1   In a 2022 online poll of 11,212 people, 76.16 per cent of autistic respondents stated they exclusively use identity-first language when referring to their autism. (Chris Bonnello, www.autisticnotweird.com)

2   Heyworth, M. 'Introduction to Autism, Part 4: The Autism Spectrum is not Linear', *https://reframingautism.org.au/introduction-to-autism-part-4-the-autism-spectrum-is-not-linear/*

3   Burgess, R. 'Understanding the spectrum: A comic strip explanation', *https://the-art-of-autism.com/understanding-the-spectrum-a-comic-strip-explanation/*

4   The Chimerical Capuchin, 'Why you're probably thinking of autism wrong', *https://thechimericalcapuchin.com/why-youre-probably-thinking-of-autism-wrong/*

5   Milton, D. E. M. (2012). On the ontological status of autism: The 'double empathy problem'. *Disability & Society, 27(6)*, 883–887

6   Statistics have generally suggested the boy-to-girl ratio is either 4:1 or 3:1, and 2:1 for autistic people who also have an intellectual disability: Loomes, R., Hull, L. and Mandy, W. (2017). What Is the Male-to-Female Ratio in Autism Spectrum Disorder? A Systematic Review and Meta-Analysis. *Journal of the American Academy of Child & Adolescent Psychiatry, 56(6)*, 466–474

7   Autistic Girls Network. (2022). Autism, Girls and Keeping It All Inside, *https://autisticgirlsnetwork.org/wp-content/uploads/2022/03/Keeping-it-all-inside.pdf;* Hull, L., Petrides, K. and Mandy, W. (2020). The Female Autism Phenotype and Camouflaging: A Narrative Review *Journal of Autism and Developmental Disorders, 7*, 306–317

8   Russell, G., Stapley, S., Newlove-Delgado, T., Salmon, A., White, R., Warren, F., Pearson, A. and Ford, T. (2022). Time trends in autism diagnosis over 20 years: a UK population-based cohort study. *Journal of Child Psychology and Psychiatry, 63(6)*, 674–682

9   Hess, P. (2022). Autism's sex bias disappears after tracking trajectories, *Spectrum News, https://www.spectrumnews.org/news/autisms-sex-bias-disappears-after-tracking-trajectories/#:~:text=The%20team%20behind%20the%20new,and%20girls%20with%20the%20condition*

10 Russell, G., Stapley, S., Newlove-Delgado, T., Salmon, A., White, R., Warren, F., Pearson, A. and Ford, T. (2022). Time trends in autism diagnosis over 20 years: a UK population-based cohort study. *Journal of Child Psychology and Psychiatry, 63(6),* 674–682

11 McCrossin, R. (2022). Finding the True Numbers of Females with Autistic Spectrum Disorder by Estimating the Biases in Initial Recognition and Clinical Diagnosis. *Children. 9(2),* 272

12 Jamison, R., Bishop, S. L., Huerta, M., and Halladay, A. K. (2017). The clinician perspective on sex differences in autism spectrum disorders, *Autism, 21(6),* 772–784

13 Yellow Ladybugs and the Department of Education and Training Victoria, (2018), Spotlight on Girls with Autism, available at *https://www.yellowladybugs.com.au/school*

14 Lawson, W. (2020). Adaptive Morphing and Coping with Social Threat in Autism: An Autistic Perspective. *Journal of Intellectual Disability – Diagnosis and Treatment, 8(8),* 519–526.

15 *https://www.squarepegroundwhole.com.au/episodes/the-elephant-in-the-room*

16 Inspired by Dr Siobhan Lamb Square Peg, Round Whole Podcast episode

17 *https://therapistndc.org/masking-goals-autistic-middle-school-girls/*

18 Yellow Ladybugs. (2016). 'Yellow Ladybugs Protection of the Rights of the Child'. (9 October). *https://www.yellowladybugs.com.au/img/Yellow%20Ladybugs%20Protection%20of %20the%20Rights%20of%20the%20Child.docx*

19 Syson, Z. and Gore Langton E. (2015). 'Simple Strategies for Supporting Children with Pathological Demand Avoidance at School'. *https://www.pdasociety.org.uk/wp-content/ uploads/2020/01/Positive-PDA-Booklet.pdf*

20 Gifted 2E Support. (2023). *https://giften2esupport.com.au*

21 School Refusal: Children and Teenagers. *https://raisingchildren.net.au/school-age/school-learning/school-refusal/school-refusal*

22 *https://www.amaze.org.au/understand-autism/about-autism/mental-health/*

23 Sedgewick, F., Leppanen, J., Tchanturia, K. (2020). Gender differences in mental health prevalence in autism. *Advances in Autism*

24 McCrossin, R. (2022). Finding the True Numbers of Females with Autistic Spectrum Disorder by Estimating the Biases in Initial Recognition and Clinical Diagnosis. *Children. 9(2),* 272

25 Russell, G., Stapley, S., Newlove-Delgado, T., Salmon, A., White, R., Warren, F., Pearson, A. and Ford, T. (2022). Time trends in autism diagnosis over 20 years: a UK population-based cohort study. *Journal of Child Psychology and Psychiatry, 63(6),* 674 -682

26 Lai, M.C., Kassee, C., Besney, R., Bonato, S., Hull, L., Mandy, W., Szatmari, P., Ameis, S.H. (2019). Prevalence of co-occurring mental health diagnoses in the autism population: a systematic review and meta-analysis. *Lancet Psychiatry, 6(10),* 819–829

27 Blanchard, A., Chihuri, S., DiGuiseppi, C.G., Guohua, L. (2021). Risk of Self-harm in Children and Adults with Autism Spectrum Disorder: A Systematic Review and Meta-analysis. *JAMA Netw Open, 4(10),* e2130272

28 *https://www.spectrumnews.org/news/psychiatric-conditions-hospitalize-almost-one-in-four-autistic-women-by-age-25/*

29 *https://www.amaze.org.au/understand-autism/about-autism/mental-health/*

30 Hirvikoski, T., Boman, M., Chen, Q., D'Onofrio, B.M., Mittendorfer-Rutz, E., Lichtenstein, P., Bölte, S., Larsson, H. (2020). Individual risk and familial liability for suicide attempt and suicide in autism: a population-based study. *Psychol Med, 50(9),*1463–1474

31 Raymaker, et al. (2020). 'Having All of Your Internal Resources Exhausted Beyond Measure and Being Left with No Clean-Up Crew': Defining Autistic Burnout. *Autism in Adulthood, 2(2),* 132–143; Higgins, et al. (2021). Defining autistic burnout through experts by lived experience: Grounded Delphi method investigating #AutisticBurnout, *Autism, 25(8),* 2356–2369

32 *https://www.dralicenicholls.com/wp-content/uploads/2021/09/The-Autistic-Burnout-Symptom-Checklist-ABSC.pdf*

33 van Steensel, F., Bogels, S., Perrin, S. (2011). Anxiety Disorders in Children and Adolescents with Autistic Spectrum Disorders: A Meta-Analysis, *Clinical Child and Family Psychology Review, 14(3),* 302–317

34 Meier, S., Petersen, L., Schendel, D., Mattheisen, M., Mortensen, P., Mors, O. (2015). Obsessive-Compulsive Disorder and Autism Spectrum Disorders: Longitudinal and Offspring Risk. *Plos One, 10(11),* e10141703

35 Solmi, et al. (2021). Trajectories of autistic social traits in childhood and adolescence and disordered eating behaviours at age 14 years: a UK general population cohort study. *Journal of Child Psychology and Psychiatry, 62(1),* 75–85

36 *https://www.butterfly.org.au*

37 Blanchard, A., Chihuri, S., DiGuiseppi, C., Guohua, L. (2021). Risk of Self-harm in Children and Adults With Autism Spectrum Disorder: A Systematic Review and Meta-analysis. *JAMA Netw Open, 4(10),* e2130272

38 Chen, M., Pan, T., Lan, W., Hsu, J., Huang, K., Su, T., Li, C., Lin, W., Wei, H., Chen, T., Bai, Y. (2017). Risk of Suicide Attempts Among Adolescents and Young Adults With Autism Spectrum Disorder: A Nationwide Longitudinal Follow-Up Study. *Journal of Clinical Psychiatry, 78(9)*, e1174–1179

39 *https://www.suicideresponseproject.com/*

40 *https://mhfa.com.au/*

41 *https://disability.royalcommission.gov.au/system/files/2021-10/Research%20Report%20-%20 Police%20responses%20to%20people%20with%20disability.pdf*

42 This is not an exhaustive list.

43 *https://www.youtube.com/watch?v=sc2xJlTO23c*

44 *https://www.spectrumnews.org/news/girls-autism-high-risk-sexual-abuse-large-study-says/*

45 *https://au.reachout.com/relationships/friendships*

46 Pecora, L. A., Hancock, G., Hooley, M., Demmer, D. H., Attwood, T., Mesibov, G. B., and Stokes, M. A. (2020). Gender identity, sexual orientation and adverse sexual experiences in autistic females. *Molecular Autism, 11(1)*, 1–57

47 Pecora, L. A., Hancock, G., Hooley, M., Demmer, D. H., Attwood, T., Mesibov, G. B., and Stokes, M. A. (2020). Gender identity, sexual orientation and adverse sexual experiences in autistic females. *Molecular Autism, 11(1)*, 1–57

48 *https://headspace.org.au/explore-topics/supporting-a-young-person/sexuality-and-sexual-identity/*

49 Gilmour, L., Schalomon, P. M., and Smith, V. (2012). Sexuality in a community based sample of adults with autism spectrum disorder. *Research in Autism Spectrum Disorders, 6(1)*, 313–318; George, R., and Stokes, M. A. (2018). Sexual Orientation in Autism Spectrum Disorder. *Autism Research, 11(1)*, 133–141

50 Barnett, J. P. and Maticka-Tyndale, E. (2015). Qualitative Exploration of Sexual Experiences Among Adults on the Autism Spectrum: Implications for Sex Education. *Perspectives on Sexual and Reproductive Health, 47(4)*, 171–179

51 Van Der Miesen, A. I. R., Hurley, H., Bal, A. M. and de Vries, A. L. C. (2018). Prevalence of the Wish to be of the Opposite Gender in Adolescents and Adults with Autism Spectrum Disorder. *Archives of Sexual Behavior, 47(8)*, 2307–2317

INDEX

A

L

Lamb, Dr Siobhan 135
language used 7–8, 18
    power of 18
    stigmatising and negative 18
lateral thinking 28
learning disabilities 165–6
LGBTQIA+ community
    autistic people and 230, 243, 246–7
    'coming out', how to provide support 251–3
    common stressful experiences 244
    Double Rainbow community 230, 243
    fluid preferences 243
    glossary of terms 253–4
    support services 251–2
lighting, sensitivity to 44, 47, 50, 115, 179
loneliness 84, 197, 273, 279, 280
low self-esteem 18

M

Marshall, Chantell 143
masking 16, 62, 226
    burdens of 34
    common traits of high-maskers 36–7
    examples 34
    impacts 35
    meaning 34
    meltdowns and 50
    misconceptions arising due to 37
    unconscious acts, as 35
meltdowns 16, 49, 50–1, 62
    after school 89
    communication, as 72
    cycle, part of 72
    involuntary 50, 51
    masking and 50
    planning for 51
    triggers and signs 50
memory, good 28
Menon, Sandhya 9, 84–5, 188
    The Brain Forest 267
    interview 223–7
mental health 186

complex *see* complex mental health
crisis *see* crisis times
    hospitalisation 186
    protective measures, building 184, 222
    self-harm *see* self-harm
    suicide *see* suicide attempts; suicide ideation
Mental Health First Aid Australia 218
minority stress 191, 207, 246, 248
misophonia 103, 111
Mudridge, JayJay 9, 11–13

N

NDIS system 41
nervous system
    parasympathetic 55
    sympathetic 55
neuro-accessibility 24
    school environments 24
neuro-affirming
    care and therapy 23
    community member thoughts 25–7
    language 16
    meaning 23–4
neurodivergent 17
    exploring your neurodivergence 262, 287–8
    meaning 19
    voices 26
neurodiversity 12, 16
    meaning 19
neurokin 4, 36
neuromajority 19
neurominority 19
    inclusion of 85
neurotypical
    being a good ally 288–90
    majority 16, 19
    meaning 19
'neurotypical passing' 23
Nicholls, Dr Alice 199
noise-cancelling headphones 47, 50, 94
non-speaking 11
non-verbal-vocal 11

Printed in the USA
CPSIA information can be obtained
at www.ICGtesting.com
LVHW010213290124
769808LV00021B/52